MW01056134

HAND TO HAND

H2H

COMBAT

MODERN ARMY COMBATIVES

GREG THOMPSON
AND
KID PELIGRO

INVISIBLE CITIES PRESS • MONTPELIER, VERMONT

I want to thank my Special Forces friends and families for their support, without them I would not be where I am today.

This book is dedicated to the men and women of the Armed Forces, and their families, for all their sacrifices.

Greg Thompson

Special thanks to Patriot Materials for their Body armor kit.
www.patriotmaterials.com

Invisible Cities Press
50 State Street
Montpelier, VT 05602
www.invisiblecitiespress.com

Copyright © 2006 by Greg Thompson and Kid Peligro
All rights reserved. This book, or any part thereof, may not be reproduced in any form without permission from the publisher.

Cataloging-in-Publication Data available from the Library of Congress

ISBN 1-931229-43-0

Anyone practicing the techniques in this book does so at his or her own risk. The authors and the publisher assume no responsibility for the use or misuse of information contained in this book or for any injuries that may occur as a result of practicing the techniques contained herein. The illustrations and text are for informational purposes only. It is imperative to practice these holds and techniques under the strict supervision of a qualified instructor. Additionally, one should consult a physician before embarking on any demanding physical activity.

Printed in the United States
Book design by Peter Holm, Sterling Hill Productions

CONTENTS

GROUND TECHNIQUES

CLINCH AND TAKEDOWN — OFFENSE AND DEFENSE

WEAPON TRANSITIONS, TAKEAWAYS, AND BASIC KNIFE

STRIKING

APPENDIX

FOREWORD
by Matt Larson

In 1995, when the Commander of the 2nd Ranger Battalion ordered us to reinvigorate the martial arts training within the battalion, we quickly uncovered serious problems within the Army's existing Combatives program. There was the general feeling among the Rangers that the techniques would not work and that it was a waste of valuable training time. In general, the Rangers would rather have been shooting, road marching or anything else that they felt could actually benefit them.

During that time, the Army had a Combatives manual, FM 21-150 (1992), but had no program to produce qualified instructors and lacked a sturdy system for implementing the training within units. All they had was a vague approach that left it to the local commander's discretion. Most soldiers laughed at the Combatives techniques they were taught in basic training. Due to this indifference, the unit instructor became whatever martial arts hobbyist happened to be in that unit, and the training narrowed down to whatever civilian martial arts those people had studied during their time off duty. In most units, there was no training at all. This was the case in the Ranger Regiment—unless the small unit leader happened to practice martial arts, there was almost no Combative training.

When we began to look for a better method, the instructors within the battalion practiced a variety of traditional martial arts: Karate, Jiu-Jitsu, Ninjitsu, Boxing, Wrestling etc. Perhaps because we had representatives from so many different martial arts, and because all of us had experienced the failure of trying to teach our particular martial art to our units, there was a general understanding that none of us had the answer.

J. Robinson, the head coach of the University of Minnesota wrestling program, himself a Vietnam era Ranger who had coached our battalion operations officer at the University of Iowa, came out to evaluate the emerging program and gave some valuable advice. He recognized that a successful program must have a competitive aspect in order to motivate soldiers to train and that it must include "live" sparring in order to be useful in cultivating a Combative culture. We began to develop a program based around wrestling, boxing and the various other martial arts we had learned, such as Judo and Muay Thai. Eventually, after looking at many different styles, we sent several men to train at the Gracie Jiu-Jitsu Academy in Torrance, California.

The Jiu-Jitsu taught at the Gracie Academy fitted many of the battalions needs. It was easy to learn, had a competitive form, and was proven effective within the arena of Mixed Martial Arts fighting. It did however have some problems. Gracie Jiu-Jitsu was principally designed for the venue that had made it famous, one-on-one arena fighting. Also, sportive Jiu-Jitsu had great potential to change the art into something not oriented toward fighting at all.

Rorion and Royce Gracie made three trips to the battalion over the next couple of years, and I also went to Torrance with a couple of others to study. During this time within the battalion, we developed the drill based training program that has become an essential element in the Modern Army Combatives (MAC) program.

The basic idea is that, since commanders have many competing priorities when it comes to training their units, any Combatives program that competes for training time with, for example, shooting, is doomed to failure. A successful Combatives program must mold around the other elements of the unit's training program. By developing a system based on drills, with each drill designed to engrain the foundational concepts of the system, small unit leaders can train Combatives in addition to their previously structured physical training program without displacing other important elements, such as running and other forms of PT. With this approach, Combatives can become an integral part of every Soldier's normal day.

As the system matured, we began to realize what made the Brazilian Jiu-Jitsu techniques work; namely, that you could practice them at full speed against a completely resistant opponent. This method can mold itself to any situation—techniques that do not work are quickly abandoned for those that do. We also began to draw from other martial arts that share aspects of this "live" training in order fill the tactical gaps of pure Gracie Jiu-Jitsu. The classic Gracie plan of taking them down and submitting them works well in the arena, but in the real world, the tactics must fit the situation; this basic "rice and beans" approach to taking the opponent down and finishing them on the ground wasn't enough for our needs.

As the program grew technically, its success catapulted it beyond the battalion. At first it moved to the rest of the Ranger Regiment, then throughout the infantry and eventually, with the publishing of the new Field Manual FM 3-25.150 (2002), it became doctrine throughout the Army.

As we began to explore the various training methods of the other "feeder arts", the ways they complemented each other and exposed each other's weaknesses became clear. The concept of positional dominance from Jiu-Jitsu expanded to the other ranges of combat and blended with techniques from wrestling, boxing, Muay Thai and Judo, to name just a few. We also incorporated expert weapons fighting, as taught by the Dog Brothers, with western martial arts and our own personal experience from years in the infantry and actual combat. By September 11th, 2001 we had finally developed a totally integrated system of Close Quarters Combat and laid a solid foundation from which to learn further lessons from the battlefields to come.

By this time, we had already established what would become the U.S. Army Combatives School at Ft. Benning, Georgia. We had already determined the first two levels of Combatives Instructor qualification, which at that time was primarily based on Mixed Martial Arts competitions fused with the prevailing wisdom on Close Quarters Battle (CQB).

When fighting started in Afghanistan, we began to conduct post action interviews with Soldiers who had experienced hand-to-hand combat. We created procedures and an interview format that drew out important lessons that might otherwise be missed in a simple narrative. Among some of the many questions that we asked: What equipment was the soldier wearing? What was the tactical situation? In the years since then, we have conducted hundreds of these interviews and adjusted the curriculum to the new lessons learned. For instance, every hand-to-hand fight we have documented has involved grappling, but not a single one has involved only striking (although, striking is always part of grappling). Also, around thirty percent of the fights end with gunshots. Fighting in an environment where everyone is armed means that the fight is most frequently over who controls the weapons.

At the same time we have continued to examine other sources for techniques. From the Brazilian Jiu-Jitsu world, Royce Gracie has remained a crucial source for some units. Romero "Jacare" Cavalcante has been an invaluable resource for the cadre at the Combatives School. Marcelo Alonso, Relson Gracie and Rigan Machado have each contributed, as have many others too numerous to name here.

We have tapped into other resources as well. Wrestling and Judo expertise from various sources, Muay Thai from Manu Ntoh, David Rogers and Greg Nelson, weapons fighting from Marc Denny of the Dog Brothers and western martial artists such as John Clemens.

Local experts at posts throughout the Army have helped this program along immensely. Those who have been acute enough to know where innovation is needed and open minded enough to understand that the Army's training program, due to its unique needs, must differ from the training regimen at civilian schools, have contributed immensely. Greg Thompson, in particular, has been one of the principle people involved in that capacity.

Greg has been the principle teacher of the MAC program at Ft. Bragg for the last several years. With the 82nd Airborne Division and the home of the Special Forces there, Ft. Bragg has been a hotbed for lessons learned directly from the battlefields. Greg, who literally has thousands of students making numerous trips to and from the war zones, has been at the forefront of capturing these lessons and developing training strategies and techniques from them.

In order to improve the hand-to-hand fighting ability of every Soldier in a unit, it is necessary to systematically develop skills, movement patterns and a strong understanding of fight strategy. The basic techniques described in this book are a blueprint for doing just that. This is the method we use in our first two instructor training courses. Beyond the basic techniques, which must be proscriptive by the nature of the challenge of teaching over a million students, the training must become conceptual, more how to train the specific technique. These techniques should be taken as examples of the type of strategies that work and should point you in the right direction. The nature of today's military conflicts - the equipment we may be wearing, the missions we find ourselves tasked with – are unique to the battlefield and are constantly changing. To meet these demands, effective Combatives training must be an ever-evolving process. This book will point you in the right direction to begin that process.

Matt Larson is widely considered to be the father of Modern Army Combatives.

Modern Army Combatives Program (1) from army Combatives Manual

"The defining characteristic of a Warrior is the willingness to close with the enemy."

Realistic Effectiveness in the battlefield:

Army Combatives were developed with practical and effective applications in mind. Using the feedback from post action interviews of soldiers from successes in Afghanistan to Kosovo, adjustments have been made to the curriculum to best represent the latest and most efficient way to fight.

The Army Combatives Bottom Line:

"The demands of training must mirror the demands of combat. If the two are different, it is the training standards that are wrong."

INTRODUCTION

WHAT IS MODERN ARMY COMBATIVES?

Modern Army Combatives was initially created by the Rangers, and further developed by Matt Larson, as a way to elevate soldiers to the next level of hand-to-hand combat. They found that the hand-to-hand techniques previously practiced did not satisfy the real needs of the soldiers on the battlefield.

HOW SHOULD A PERSON LEARNING MAC AND H2H THINK AND ACT?

The Modern Army Combatives is the first phase of this book; these are the basic techniques taught to today's soldiers so they can learn the fundamental principles of hand-to-hand and build from them. A lot of other programs fail because they don't teach the soldiers how to spar and further develop their techniques. They'll teach something like, "Here is an arm bar, and here is a sequence from a common reaction to the move, when he does this then you do this." Because a fight is always changing, you can't really teach someone how to fight effectively without giving them a set of moves. You have to develop an instinct for fighting, which means that you have to practice grappling and striking.

This H2H Combatives manual will illustrate the Modern Army Combatives aspect of training. This is the same thing that Helio Gracie did in his basic Jiu-Jitsu training classes. Matt Larson adapted this for the Army in the Army Combatives Level I and II. When Matt Larson started training Jiu-Jitsu with Royce Gracie and Rorion Gracie, he thought: "Here is a system which will allow me to quickly train a soldier and give him the strong fighting tactics of Jiu-Jitsu." By fight tactics, I mean a concept of sequences of techniques and reactions, a tactical concept consisting of several important features. First, in learning fight tactics, you need to know what position requires what response. And second, you should know at least two chokes and one or two submissions. With this, an average individual will at least have the necessary thought processes, and know the game plan of how to move and respond. Taught correctly, it should be effective and deeply ingrained within the student's minds. The previous systems gave them only a set of kicks, punches and tricks, and because of this, they lacked the necessary fight tactics. When the actual fight came, they would simply go toe-to-toe with their enemy. If the enemy were more athletic or stronger than them, the soldier would fail. This training was unsatisfactory. With the Army Combatives System, the tactics circumvent what 99% of the people do in a fight (exchange punches) and instead replace it with an idea and a tactical system that would emphasize closing the distance, taking the enemy down and securing the weapon. A soldier trained with our method will be able to choose what to do, whether a submission or a shot!

This H2H Combatives manual not only teaches you the Combatives Level I & II with the basic Jiu-Jitsu, but it goes one step further by taking the fundamentals that you learn in the M.A.C. and showing you how to gravitate to a dominant position. This H2H book shows a combination of the basic techniques taught to the regular Army, and H2H, which is what I teach to the Special Forces and has emphasis in weapon retention and control. Using feedback from real soldiers, I modified and perfected the H2H program into the ultimate combative fighting system. A grappler is a weapon transition expert and doesn't always know it. When you introduce a primary or secondary weapon into a *fight situation*, you need to have enough room so that the enemy can't grab you. If he grabs you, then you are now grappling for the weapon. You are either going to take it away from him, or he is going to take it away from you. The person that can keep or retain the weapon is the ultimate winner of that scrimmage; and a grappler is generally the best at this.

Now, in modern warfare, fixed objects are around the soldier at all times (walls, chairs, doors, etc.), and the rooms they fight in are not big rings, like the U.F.C. Octagon, in which you can move around the circle and fight like Chuck Liddell and others. In today's modern warfare situations, the surrounding fixed objects make it harder to stop somebody from grabbing you. And once they grab you, you need to know the principles of H2H Combatives that deal with the clinch from the foundation of Modern Army Combatives. The H2H expands and teaches you: "Hey, when he clinches me up, I need to have my head on the weapon side. That way, I can get leverage over that weapon! If I am going to take a weapon from him, I need to put my head on the weapon side. That way, I'll gain more leverage. If I hit the ground, I need to develop the instinctive movement to go to a mounted position or to a side-mount position so he doesn't end up with his legs around me. If he takes me down, I need to use my feet and legs to gain leverage over him so I can safely transition to a weapon."

Granted, when you introduce a weapon in a Combative situation, the attacker may not know much and still take you down and tightly hug you. He may end up in an advantageous position and still just hug you, trying to control you in this way without even realizing that he has a great position. He may end up side mounted or mounted on you and not even realize that he is in the dominant position. You could easily pull your weapon out and have an instant kill – if you are able to shoot his spinal cord or shoot him right between the eyes, the guy is done - but the soldier needs more tactics than that. The soldier doesn't run into a building and say, "I am just going to run in and shoot this guy." A soldier is given tactics, even though the person that he is fighting may not have tactics. The soldier needs to have tactics and he needs to understand fight tactics.

In these weapon transitions, a crucial aspect of fight tactics, you learn how to use the fundamentals of Jiu-Jitsu when transitioning to your secondary weapon, no matter if it is a blade or a gun. And more often than not, these fundamentals are going to be crucial; in a fight situation, the instant you bring a semi-automatic pistol into the equation and the barrel or slide gets grabbed by the enemy, the gun will likely discharge and damage the enemy's hand, but if the slide doesn't cycle properly the pistol will jam after one shot. When this happens, the gun becomes a blunt object and you are once again fighting hand-to-hand. But if you can get to a dominant position *from any other position*, you can clear the gun completely free and out of his hand, so instead of only getting one shot, you can fire multiple shots. It is not always just him that you have to worry about; even if you take care of him and free your gun, he may have a buddy that follows him with another firearm. So you need to be able to shoot him as well. In modern warfare Combative situations, the winner of the fight is the one that ends up with the gun, and that is generally the better Combatives fighter. The fundamental techniques and principles that you are going to learn in H2H are going to help you hurry up and effectively eliminate your enemy in whatever situation you're in, with the least amount of risk to yourself. It will give you a chance to shoot him when you're on your back from the guard, and then, during the same confrontation, shoot somebody else who is coming at you.

Someone who gets through the fundamentals of this book will learn how to grapple and will know many powerful techniques. When you get tackled from the front, side or back, and you hit the ground, you will know how to transition properly either on the ground or, even better, stop the takedown. You'll learn the proper way of executing this, the clinch, which will increase your odds of effectively getting your weapon out and keeping it in your possession. Or, if you have taken a weapon away from someone else, you will know the game plan and a set of leverage tactics that will give you an edge in the fight.

What is Important to Learn to Win in the hand-to-hand Combat

The most important thing to have if you want to be good at these techniques is the desire to train. Whatever you're teaching them, whether it's Jiu-Jitsu, Muay Thai or wrestling, you need to make it enjoyable so that they want to come back or train on their own. Beyond that, I emphasize that it's important to learn all ranges of fighting and the tactics of transitioning and retaining your weapon. Fighting is fighting—whether you are fighting for a weapon or fighting with your hands, the principles of leverage always apply. That is why you are learning these techniques. I try to emphasize two important aspects; I try to teach Jiu-Jitsu, while always reminding them that a weapon can be introduced, and that it will be an important factor in the fight. This helps the students to relate better because it focuses on real hand-to-hand Jiu-Jitsu combat, and not the competition environment. I emphasize the real element of survival because these guys are literally fighting for their lives.

In this book, there are certain tactics and techniques that it will help to know. If someone doesn't know these principles and tries to go toe-to-toe with a bigger, more athletic person, he may end up losing his weapon because he doesn't understand these fighting dynamics. This book will teach you weapon takeaways and other weapon training techniques, so in a real situation you can securely keep your weapon in your possession at all times. Since our tactics are evaluated, and improved upon, by feedback we get from our students that enter Real Combat Situations, these are not just imaginary scenarios. Because these guys are entering the field in incredibly difficult situations, when a technique doesn't work quite right, we examine it and then improve it.

How to Learn

It saves time teaching the H2H™ combative if the student has MAC level I and II, because we often do not have the time to spend teaching this. First, learn how to fight with leverage in mind, training against standing objects and objects on the ground, and from mugging from behind drills, with no weapons. Once you are programmed with the right tactics in mind, add weapon transitions. Then, once you can transition to your weapon instinctively, add the kit. The kit is a hindrance; it will make it hard to move in some situations. But this doesn't mean that the kit is a total disadvantage; it can be used as a weapon. If you can mount, side mount, or knee mount the enemy, the extra weight will help to crush them. Additionally, with all the sharp objects that you have in your kit, if he ends up on top of you, you can grab his face and grind it into your kit. This will rip him up and change his focus.

After training, you may decide to change how you carry your transitional weapons. Can you get to your knife with both hands? If your pistol is carried high on your chest, can you safely pull it out in a clinch without losing leverage? Can you get to it when sitting in a vehicle or on the ground? In a Real Combat Situation, or on the streets? A fight is a mugging: you will mug him or he will mug you. In most street fights, someone has the first swing and it won't be expected. He won't hold up his fists in a fighting stance he will just come out with a surprise swing. If you are in combat, and get tackled from behind, that is a mugging. The knowledge you learn in training will help mold instinctive movements in all areas; standing, on the ground, or against an object. You must create scenarios that are realistic and educational, because in training it is OK to lose. This way, you can learn about yourself and realistically gauge your abilities.

Authors

Greg Thompson

Greg Thompson is a 4th level certified Combatives Instructor in the military. Greg is proficient in martial arts, he holds a Black Belt in Gracie Jiu-Jitsu from Royce Gracie. He achieved this after 12 years of training; in addition, he is an Instructor Kru in Muay Thai and Black Belt in Karate and Tae Kwon Do. Greg has been training the Army since 1998. In addition, after September 11, 2001, Greg was contracted as a Federal Defense Tactics and Air Marshal Hand-to-hand instructor in Artesia, New Mexico for one year.

The owner of Team R.O.C. (Reality Of Combat), Greg has produced a number of professional MMA fighters and is currently active in training and developing fighters. Greg is also an inventor; he is the creator of the "Defenseband," ™ a watchband that can be used as a restraining device that allows you to choke somebody, and he is also the creator of the "Spider-Ti," ™ a human restraining system. Greg lives and teaches in North Carolina - www.h2h.us

About Greg Thompson

Two words describe Greg Thompson: ability and wisdom. As a martial arts instructor, Greg Thompson is a rarity. He has the natural physical and mental abilities of a world-class fighter and has the skills to back it up. His wisdom as an instructor is unsurpassed, having exceptional skills in all areas of martial arts, from weapons to all ranges of fighting. With all this said, what makes him special is his ability to shift from fighter to student to instructor with amazing grace, humility and confidence.

His unique talents of inventing have allowed Greg to make one of the most effective self-defense tools ever made, the Defenseband. Without a doubt it is the most devastating non-lethal self-defense tool for the individual I have ever seen. It is with great pride I call Greg one of my students, friend and instructors.

Scott Francis, (former Thai Boxing Champion)

Kid Peligro

Kid Peligro is a 2nd degreeBlack Belt in Brazilian Jiu-Jitsu and the winner of two World Masters titles. He is a top columnist for magazines all over the world like *Throwdown* and *Grappling* Magazines in the U.S.A., *Gracie Magazine* in Brazil and *Fighter Magazine* in Sweden. Kid is the author or co-author of an unprecedented number of best selling books like *The Gracie Way, Brazilian Jiu-Jitsu The Essential Guard, Brazilian Jiu-Jitsu Self-Defense Techniques, From First Down to Touchdown, Submission Grappling Techniques*, and *Superfit*. His writing skills are precise and flexible enough so that he excels in translating the thoughts and insights of the co-author's knowledge into words, placing him in high demand for high caliber book projects.

THE ASSISTANT
Aitor Canup

Aitor Canup started training MMA under Greg Thompson in 1996. He is a Muay Thai instructor who also holds a Brown Belt in Brazilian Jiu-Jitsu from Royce Gracie. Aitor also teaches Level II Instruction in the Modern Army Combatives Program. Since July 2002, working under Greg Thompson, Aitor has conducted daily 8 hour training sessions with Army Special Forces units stationed at Fort Bragg, NC. A professional MMA fighter and coach, Aitor has fought in some of the world's best events such as K1's Rumble on The Rock and King of the Cage.

MODERN ARMY COMBATIVES

LEVEL I

Modern Army Combatives I teaches you the first 19 moves. MAC I encompasses the fundamentals of hand-to-hand fighting. You are taught the same moves that every recruit in the U.S. Army learns as part of their hand-to-hand combat training. Additionally you will learn basic fight strategy and concepts that give you a footprint on how to survive a combative fighting situation.

MAC I is a quick and effective training program for those who need to better their fighting skills in a short amount of time.

STANDING IN BASE

Being able to stand up in base (feet slightly wider than the shoulders, knees bent, your weight equally distributed between both legs and your back should be straight and tilted slightly forward) is critical whether you are a soldier operating on the field or someone being attacked in a street fight. The elements of properly standing up in base include defending your face and body from being struck by your opponent and maintaining proper balance and base throughout the movement. You must maintain your balance and defensive posture even in the event that your opponent charges you during the movement. Always stand with your weapon side away from the enemy.

1 Greg is on the ground with Peter standing in front of him ready to strike. To protect himself from being struck by a punch or especially a kick, Greg bends his left leg and plants the left foot on the mat. Greg places his left arm bent at the elbow in front of his face. The elbow rests against his left knee, creating a barrier from his left foot through his left hand, blocking any strikes from reaching his face and torso. Greg uses the right arm as a brace with the right hand planted on the mat just back of his right hip. Greg's right leg is slightly extended forward with the foot ready to strike to keep Peter away. Notice that Greg's body is turned slightly to his right to present a smaller target for Peter.

2 To stand up, Greg needs to create some distance between himself and Peter, otherwise Peter can strike any time during the standing motion. Greg pushes off his left foot and right hand and raises his hips off the ground. Pushing off his right hand, Greg swings his body forward as he extends his right leg, thrusting his foot at Peter's forward knee. The strike forces Peter to retreat, creating the distance and time for Greg to stand up. Notice that Greg will use this type of strike to maintain a safe distance from Peter. Any time Peter gets close enough that he can strike Greg with a kick or a punch Greg will kick Peter's knee and force him back.

3 Still bracing off his left foot and right arm, Greg coils his right leg back. He uses the recoil motion from the kick to help pull the leg under his body until he can plant the right foot on the ground slightly past his hand. Notice that Greg has a perfect 3-point stance here: his weight is distributed evenly between his feet and right hand. Should Peter charge him and try to push him back, Greg will be able to keep his stance with his right arm and leg as a brace. In the event that Peter tries to pull him forward Greg can resist by pushing off his left foot and leaning back. Notice that at all times Greg has his left arm in front of his face protecting it and he is always looking at Peter ready to react in case Peter moves to strike.

4 Greg raises his body and reaches a fighting stance, ready to engage Peter.

OPTIONAL TECHNIQUES

107

ESCAPING THE MOUNT:
Trap and roll

The mounted position is perhaps one of the worst positions one can find oneself during a fight. Being able to quickly and effectively escape from it is a must. The "upa" or bridge escape is a basic maneuver that must be mastered by anyone with plans of surviving an attack. The key elements to escaping the mount trap and roll are the use of the bridge to propel your opponent's weight forward and to completely block one side of your opponent to take away his ability to brace and stop your rolling motion.

1 Peter is mounted on Greg with his weight forward on the right arm. His right hand grips Greg's throat and the left arm is cocked and ready to strike. Greg's first concern is the choking pressure on his throat. He grabs Peter's right wrist with his right hand. The palm of the hand pushes to the left to release some of the pressure and all five fingers are cupped on the outside of the wrist to trap it. With his left hand, Greg grabs Peter's right arm just behind the elbow. Notice that Greg has great defensive posture: his left elbow is tight against his body, blocking Peter's right leg from moving up. Having secured control over Peter's right arm, Greg loops his left foot over Peter's right calf, planting it right next to Peter's foot to trap the leg. At this point Greg has completely blocked Peter's ability to brace to his right side.

2 Greg's second concern is preventing Peter from striking his face with the left punch so he pushes off his feet and raises his hips in a bridging motion. This forces Peter to use his left arm to catch his fall. When mounted you should bridge up anytime you see your opponent cocking his arm to deliver a punch. You will project his torso forward and force him to use the arm to brace himself. At this point Peter's weight is forward resting mostly on his left arm. This pins the arm on the ground and prevents him from using it to stop the rolling motion that follows.

3 Pushing off his right foot Greg rolls over his left shoulder. As both bodies hit the ground Greg kicks the right leg over, continuing the rolling motion. Greg ends the roll inside Peter's guard with his head pressing against Peter's chest and his hands cupping Peter's biceps to prevent him from punching.

OPTIONAL TECHNIQUES

6, 59

PASSING THE GUARD

Being able to pass someone's guard is a vital skill in a battle for survival. If you are incapable of escaping an attacker's guard control and reaching his side, you allow him opportunities to submit you, strike you with heel kicks or reverse the position via a sweep, ending up on top of you. Here is one of the preferred ways to pass someone's guard in battle. It is a fundamental way to develop and build balance and the ability to counter leverage. The keys to this pass are proper posture (head and spine aligned to create a solid unit) and proper use of your weight distribution as you move through the technique.

1 Greg is inside Peter's closed guard. Greg's head is pressed against the chest and his hands cup Peter's biceps to prevent Peter from punching his face. While pushing off his arms, Greg turns his hips to his right and opens out his right leg, planting the foot back and to the right just past the line of his left foot.

a

b

c

2 Greg's turning creates a space between Peter's legs so he can slide his right hand in between his hip and Peter's left leg. Greg slides his right arm in that space and plants the right hand on the mat between his right foot and Peter's buttocks. Greg pushes off his right hand and feet to raise his torso as he brings in the right knee just under Peter's left hip. He grabs Peter's left thigh with his right arm. At this point Greg's posture is critical: he must keep a perfect straight line with his spine and neck with the head turned up to prevent a triangle attempt from Peter.

2 Greg's head and spine posture: his back is perfectly aligned with his neck and head tilted back. Also notice how Greg holds his left elbow tight against his left knee with his arm and thigh trapping Peter's right leg. Once he raises his torso he grabs the left thigh with the right arm: this is the secret to blocking the triangle. If Peter cannot move his hips up and to the side, he cannot complete the triangle lock.

3 Greg reaches with his right hand and grabs Peter's right shoulder. He then springs off his feet and stretches his legs back, pushing off the extended right leg. Greg drives his body forward as he pulls on Peter's shoulder with the right hand, stacking Peter's legs on top of his head. Greg continues to move to his own right still stacking Peter's legs onto himself. Greg kneels with his right knee pushed into Peter's left armpit.

4 Greg extends his legs back, driving his chest forward and pushing Peter's legs away. This clears his head from behind Peter's left thigh. Greg reaches side control with his chest pressed against Peter's chest. Greg secures side control by bringing his knees in close to Peter's body, taking away any space for Peter to coil his leg in and replace the guard.

REVERSE

3 & 4

Notice Greg's use of his legs and body weight to break Peter's leg barrier and pass the guard. Greg switches his pressure from one leg to the other as he maneuvers around Peter's legs, stacking them over his head in the process.

a

b

c

d

REVERSE

ALTERNATIVE

3 & 4

Alternatively, as he is stacking Peter's legs over his head, Greg may choose to slide his left arm back and grab the bottom of Peter's pants with his hand to prevent him from rolling over his shoulder and escaping the guard pass.

a

b

c

d

OPTIONAL TECHNIQUES

39, 40, 41, 44, 45, 58, 71

FOLLOW UP TECHNIQUES

Side mount-4, 5, 10, 11, 26, 28, 31, 46, 54, 65, 66, 86

SIDE CONTROL

The side control is one of the basic controlling positions in Brazilian Jiu-Jitsu. It is also an extremely important position for controlling and delivering punishment and weapon retention, transition and takeaways to the opponent on the field. The side control is a very stable position. With your chest pressing down against the opponent's chest and your arms controlling his hips and head, the side control is an ideal position to deliver strikes to the opponent without the risk of being reversed. A solid side control position involves having your legs spread to achieve a firm base and blocking your opponent's hips and head from moving, thus controlling his body.

Side control, arms on the same side:
In this side control position, Greg has both arms on the same side of Peter's body. His left elbow is tight against Peter's left ear, preventing him from moving the head. Greg's right elbow presses against Peter's left hip, preventing him from escaping the hip out to replace the guard. In this case, since both of Greg's arms are to one side, Greg needs to bring his lower knee, in this case the right knee, in tight against Peter's right hip to block his right leg from sliding under in an attempt to replace the guard. Greg's hips are down with his chest pressing down against Peter's chest.

Side control arms on opposite sides:
In this case, Greg uses an alternate arm position for the side control with one arm on each side of Peter's body. Greg's left arm remains in the same position as above with his elbow tight against Peter's left ear. However his right arm, with the hand planted on the mat next to Peter's right hip now blocks Peter's ability to coil his right leg in to try to replace the guard. In this case, since his right hand blocks the guard replacement, Greg has both legs stretched out with the hips pushing down.

OPTIONAL TECHNIQUES

5, 10, 11, 26, 28, 31, 46, 54, 65, 66, 86

ACHIEVE THE MOUNT FROM SIDE CONTROL

After controlling your opponent with the side control position, you may want to proceed to the next position in the hierarchy, the mounted position. The mount, despite being less stable than the side control, is the best position to deliver punches to the opponent's face and to apply a variety of submissions. In addition, it is another key position for weapon retention, transition and takeaways. The key to the successful transition is to first clear the elbow that is blocking your hips, then clear the legs just prior to looping your legs over. Also make sure that you maintain a stable base at all times so you don't get reversed if your opponent tries to ridge and bump over. Here we demonstrate the transition from side control to the mounted position.

1 Greg has side control on Peter. Greg's legs are stretched back and opened wide to maintain a broad base and have stability. His body is at 90° with Peter's body with his chest pressing down against Peter's chest. Greg's right arm, with the hand touching the mat next to Peter's right hip, blocks Peter from coiling his right leg in an attempt to replace the guard. Greg's left elbow touches the mat and presses against Peter's left ear. The elbow positioning here is very important, Greg's elbow should be tight against Peter's head, preventing him from moving the head and making it very difficult for Peter to move his body. Peter has good defensive position from the bottom. His left arm under Greg's right armpit is protected from any attacks and the right arm, bent at the elbow, presses against Greg's hips to maintain distance.

2 Greg now starts his transition to achieving the mounted position. His first step is to clear Peter's right arm out of the way. Greg switches his hips, driving the left knee towards the right until it clears past Peter's right elbow. Greg then drives the left leg back, pushing the knee against Peter's ribcage and forcing him to open the right arm out, clearing it out of the way.

3 Having cleared Peter's right elbow block, Greg proceeds towards the mount. He switches the hips again, driving the left knee towards the right. He makes sure his buttocks touch the ground to prevent Peter from getting his right arm back into blocking position. Greg loops the right leg back with the foot firmly planted on the mat for stability in case Peter tries to bump him off. With his right hand, Greg grabs Peter's left pants at the knee and pulls the legs towards him, making it easier for him to loop his right leg over Peter's legs.

a

b

4 Greg loops his right leg over Peter's legs, making sure to hook the heel right behind Peter's left knee. Greg continues moving over Peter and places both knees on the ground next to Peter's hips. Once he is firmly set on top of Peter, Greg opens his arms above Peter's head to maintain his balance and to be better able to maintain the position.

c

REVERSE

Notice Greg's right elbow: it is tight against Peter's left ear, taking away any space for him to move the head and escape. Also notice Greg's use of the right hand to clear Peter's legs towards him as he loops his right leg over them. It is very important for Greg to hook the heel right under the thigh so he can keep pressing Peter's legs down, making it easier for him to mount and harder for Peter to escape his hips and try to replace the guard.

a
b
c
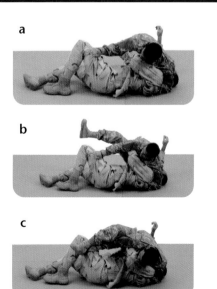

OPTIONAL TECHNIQUES

10, 11, 26, 28, 31, 46, 54, 65, 66, 86

FOLLOW UP TECHNIQUES

Mount- 7, 10, 11, 12, 26, 27, 28, 54, 65, 66, 86

ESCAPE THE MOUNT: *Shrimp to the guard*

Hopefully you will never find yourself in a fight situation with your opponent (or enemy) mounted on top of you. However a fight is a very dynamic environment and bad positions do occur. The key to surviving and winning is to be able to maintain your wits even under duress and be able to properly select and execute the proper escape. We have previously demonstrated using the trap and roll (technique #2) to escape the mount. Here we demonstrate another very effective way to escape the mount called "shrimping". Shrimping is one of the most effective ways to escape the mount and replace the guard. It is especially useful in conjunction with the trap and roll when your opponent is able to open his leg and block the roll attempt. Shrimping, much like the trap and roll, can be used as a first option to escape the mount as well.

a

b

1 Peter is mounted on Greg. Greg attempts to escape the mount with the trap and roll. He grabs Peter's right arm with both hands and pushes off his feet, raising his hips up in a bridge position and causing Peter to lean forward and use his left arm to brace. As Greg tries to roll Peter to the left, Peter is able to open his right leg out and block the roll attempt. This is the perfect moment for Greg to use the shrimping technique. Greg pushes off his right foot and moves his hips to the right as he moves his head down towards his left knee. He then places his left hand on Peter's right hip to keep the distance as he coils his left leg in, sliding the knee under Peter's right leg. Notice that Greg's left knee and left elbow touch each other to form a block from the left foot to the left hand. This stops Peter from being able to bring his right knee next to Greg's body.

c

2 Greg loops the left leg around Peter's right leg to complete one side of the escape.

OPTIONAL TECHNIQUES

2, 59

FOLLOW UP TECHNIQUES

Guard 13, 14, 15, 32, 33, 34, 35, 36, 37, 42, 43, 62, 63, 64, 65, 66, 67, 68, 69, 70

a

b

c

d

3 Greg pushes off his right foot and now escapes the hips to his left to execute the same shrimping move on the opposite side. Greg uses his right hand on Peter's left hip to create distance as he coils and brings the right leg in and around Peter's left leg. Greg then locks his feet behind Peter's back, having escaped the mount and achieving closed guard.

REVERSE

3 Notice Greg's movement on his right side. He uses his right arm to block Peter's hips, allowing the proper space for his right knee to come in front of Peter's left hip. Greg then pushes off his right foot and escapes his hips to the right so he can loop the right leg out and around Peter's left leg.

a

b

c

d

ARM PUSH AND ROLL TO THE REAR MOUNT

Many times when you are mounted on your opponent he will have his arms in front of his chest in a defensive posture. He may do so to protect his neck from chokes or to have his hands near his face to block punches. Regardless of what his motives may be, take advantage of that defense and take his back using the arm push and roll.

1 Greg is mounted on Peter. Peter has his arms in front of his chest in a defensive posture. With his right hand Greg grabs Peter's right wrist as he leans forward to put his weight on the arm. Greg uses his left hand to push Peter's right elbow to Greg's right, crossing Peter's arm in front of his own chest.

REVERSE

1 Notice how Greg drives his weight down on Peter's arm as he grabs the wrist with the right hand and pushes the elbow with the left forcing it across the body.

2 Greg drops his chest down, pressing it against the back of Peter's arm and preventing him from pulling it back across. Greg then reaches with his left arm around Peter's head until he can grab Peter's right wrist with his hand. At this point, Greg releases his right hand grip on Peter's wrist, sliding the right arm under Peter's left arm.

a

b

3 Greg slides his left knee forward towards Peter's head and raises his right knee up as he reaches the side mount. With his right hand Greg pushes down on Peter's right elbow while he pulls the wrist across with his right hand forcing Peter to turn over to his side. Greg grabs Peter's left forearm with his own right hand achieving total control over Peter's torso.

c

REVERSE

3 Notice how Greg's left knee slides forward, getting right next to Peter's head while his right leg – knee raised and the heel touching the stomach – maintains tightness and control over Peter's torso and hips.

a

b

4 Greg continues turning Peter onto his stomach by pulling the wrist and pushing the elbow until Peter is completely turned over. Greg achieves back control.

c

OPTIONAL TECHNIQUES

10, 11, 12, 26, 27,
28, 54, 65, 66, 86

FOLLOW UP TECHNIQUES

Rear mount- 9, 29, 30, 65, 66

ESCAPING THE REAR MOUNT

Perhaps the most precarious position you can find yourself in during a fight is having someone on your back with hooks. Without a clear view of your opponent's intentions, he has a great timing advantage and is free to deliver strikes to the back of your head and apply a finishing choke. If you find yourself in this situation, your first concern should be to maintain your poise and your wits. Without them you will succumb. Mastering this escape will give you the confidence that you can escape this difficult situation.

1 Peter has back control over Greg. Greg's first concern is to maintain proper defensive position and protect his neck from a choke. To do so, he wraps his left arm around the forehead and keeps the right arm bent at the elbow and tight against his chest with the hand open right under his left armpit. Notice how Greg's left arm and right hand make an impenetrable barrier for any possible choke. As soon as Peter tries to wrap his left arm around Greg's neck for a choke, he is intercepted as Greg grabs the wrist with his right hand.

2 Having secured Peter's left arm, Greg knows his escape is to the left. At this point, even if Peter wraps his right arm around Greg's neck he cannot choke him, first because he needs two arms to secure the choke and second because Greg will lean away from the right arm towards the opening for the escape. Greg wraps his left arm over Peter's left arm, trapping the elbow, and leans to the left. Greg falls to his left. He helps his cause by pushing off the right foot as he coils his right leg and extends the left. Notice that Greg still maintains control over Peter's left arm.

ANATOMY OF TECHNIQUES

K) Blood flow (Arteries)

a

b

c

3 Greg continues to lean to his left. Now pushing off the right foot, he bridges up, pushing first his head against the ground then the left shoulder. Once he has his head and shoulder on the ground Greg starts to turn to his right as if to face Peter. At this point Greg has already escaped the back control. His concern now is to stop Peter from mounting him, so Greg uses his left hand to block Peter's right leg from looping over. Greg continues to turn towards his right, pushing off both legs now, and escapes his hips away from Peter.

4 Greg coils his legs and hooks his feet inside Peter's legs under the thighs to block Peter from mounting or closing his legs around Greg's body for the closed guard. Greg turns his torso completely to the right and plants both hands on the mat.

TOP VIEW

4 Notice how Greg hooks the left foot under Peter's right thigh. This not only helps him block Peter's attempt at mounting him but it also allows Greg to push Peter's leg back to the left as he goes for the mount himself.

a

b

c

5 Pushing off his arms, Greg drives his body over the top. Once he is on top of Peter, he loops his feet around Peter's legs and reaches the mounted position.

REAR NAKED CHOKE

The rear naked choke is the most powerful and effective choke in fighting. By constricting the blood flow to the brain you can effectively render your opponent unconscious in a few seconds or you can kill him, if you hold it long enough. The rear naked choke is perhaps one of the greatest fight-ending submission holds, as a fighter can continue to fight with a broken arm or a broken foot but he cannot muster a reaction when he is passed out. We demonstrate the choke with the opponent sitting down for best viewing purposes.

1 Greg wraps his left arm around Peter's neck so his right hand can transition to a secondary weapon for retention or protection from other assailants. He makes sure his hand comes all the way past the neck to the right shoulder.

a

b

c

2 Greg bends the right arm at the elbow and brings it forward so that he can grab his own biceps with his left hand. After grabbing the biceps, Greg drives the right hand behind Peter's head, completing the choke lock. Greg makes a fist with the right hand and places it behind Peter's head. Greg brings the elbows together, as he brings his arms to his chest and drives his head forward, pressing on Peter's head for the choke.

SIDE VIEW

Notice how Greg's right hand is in a fist and not grabbing over Peter's head. The fist keeps the fingers together, making it difficult for Peter to try to break them as a last resort defense.

INCORRECT

2 Notice that it is important to lock the arms with the right arm bent instead of grabbing the biceps with the right arm extended, as this would allow the opponent to block the choke by grabbing the right wrist to prevent the hand from getting behind his head. Also incorrect is to have the right hand open and over the head instead of in a fist behind the neck: notice how Peter can reach with his left hand and grab Greg's fingers, breaking them and pulling the hand away.

a

b

c

OPTIONAL TECHNIQUES

29, 30, 65, 66

CROSS-COLLAR CHOKE FROM THE MOUNT AND GUARD

The cross-collar choke is another one of the great chokes used in combatives. The choke principles are always the same: cutting the blood flow to the brain. Although the collar choke uses the opponent's collar to assist in the mechanics, it can also work by grabbing the shoulders blades with the hands instead. The cross-collar choke can be executed from various positions. We demonstrate two: from the mount and from the closed guard.

From the mount:

1 Greg is mounted on Peter. With his left hand Greg pulls open Peter's right lapel making it easy for his right hand to slide in and grab the collar as deep as possible. Notice that Greg's right hand is open with the fingers together and the palm facing out. Greg slides the fingers inside the collar and uses the thumb on the outside to help secure the grip. Once he has his first hand in the collar, Greg plants his left hand forward above Peter's head and leans forward with his torso to maintain his balance and prevent Peter from using the trap and roll escape (technique #2).

a

b

c

2 Greg opens his right leg, shifting his hips slightly to the left and placing his weight on the left knee. This body shift creates a better angle for Greg to reach over with his left arm and insert the left thumb inside Peter's left collar to wrap the fingers on the outside and grab the collar. With both collars firmly secured, Greg tightens the choke by pulling his elbows up.

3 Greg then brings the right leg back in tight against Peter's left hip and leans forward, putting his forehead on the ground above Peter's head for both balance and to add pressure to the choke as he extends his body and drives his chest down against Peter's face. Notice that to properly tighten the choke Greg brings the elbows up and back along the side of his body instead of opening them out towards the front as it is incorrectly done sometimes by beginners.

From the closed guard:

1 The choke is applied much the same way from the closed guard. This time however, as a variation Greg slides the second hand under the left arm (first hand) instead of reaching over the top. Since he is on the bottom and proximity is very important on any choke, Greg brings Peter's chest down to him by pulling with his arms.

OPTIONAL TECHNIQUES

Guard-13, 14, 15, 32, 33, 34, 35, 36, 37,42, 43, 62, 63, 64, 65, 66, 67, 68, 69, 70
Mount-7, 10, 11, 12, 26, 27, 28, 54, 65, 66, 86

H2H

TECHNIQUE
011

BENT ARM-BAR

Another very effective submission that can be used from various positions is the bent arm-bar also known as the paint brush or the figure 4 arm-lock. In the bent arm-bar, the pain and damage is actually to the shoulder and not the elbow joint as in other arm-bars. The bent arm-bar can be used from the mount, the closed guard and side-control and many other positions. It is also good for weapon retention and takeaway.

From the mount:

The key here is to maintain control over the arm, keeping the wrist on the ground and close to the opponent's body.

1 Greg is mounted on Peter. Peter has both arms bent with the elbows close to his body and the hands protecting the face and the neck from punches and chokes. In one quick movement Greg turns his torso to his right as he drives down his left arm, grabbing Peter's left wrist with his left hand. Greg uses the weight of his torso to drive and pin the wrist to the ground. Greg ends up with his left elbow tight against Peter's left side of the face. He uses the claw grip – the four fingers and the thumb together – for maximum grip.

2 Greg slides the right hand under Peter's left arm until he reaches and grabs his own left wrist with it, securing the figure 4 lock on Peter's arm.

3 Greg brings the entire lock down along the side of Peter's torso, sliding Peter's left wrist down the mat as he lifts his own elbow up. This forces Peter's left arm up and torques the shoulder for the submission. Greg grapevines his legs on Peter's legs for control and extends his body for extra pressure on the arm.

38

SIDE VIEW

3 Notice how Greg slides Peter's wrist down the mat while lifting the elbow up to torque the arm around the shoulder. It is very important for Greg to keep Peter's wrist on the mat and the arm bent at all times for maximum pressure on the shoulder joint. If he allows the wrist to rise or the arm to extend the pressure is greatly diminished.

OPTIONAL TECHNIQUES

Mount-7, 10, 12, 26, 27, 28, 54, 65, 66, 86

ANATOMY OF TECHNIQUES

G) Bent Arm Bar Separation

Side control:

The same attack can be applied from the side control. Any time your opponent's arm is exposed in front of you is an opportunity to use this attack.

1 In this case Peter has his forearm pressing against Greg's throat to create space. Greg simply uses his left hand to grab and push down on Peter's left wrist until he pins it to the ground. Notice that as soon as he grabs the wrist Greg pushes off his left foot, raises his hips and slides his right leg back under so he can switch the hips and get chest-to-chest with Peter. This allows him to lock Peter's wrist on the ground and set up the submission. From there on the mechanics of the submission are the same. Greg slides his right arm under the left arm until he can grab his left wrist with the right hand and slides the wrist down along the side of Peter's torso while raising the elbow pressure on the shoulder.

OPTIONAL TECHNIQUES

Side control-4, 5, 10, 11, 26, 28, 31, 46, 54, 65, 66, 86

ANATOMY OF TECHNIQUES

G) Bent Arm Bar Separation

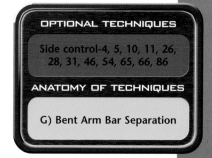

2 Here, Peter has his arm around the back of Greg's head. Greg can either wait for Peter to move his arm in front or he can reach back with his left hand to grab Peter's wrist.

STRAIGHT ARM-BAR FROM THE MOUNT

Having someone mounted on you and delivering punches is a difficult experience for even an experienced fighter to withstand. The pressure of the opponent's weight on your chest coupled with the blows makes most anyone panic and try anything to escape the position. One of the most common escape counters used (especially by inexperienced fighters) is to extend the arms and try to push the person off the top. In that case, the straight arm-bar is the perfect option leading to a quick submission. The keys to the arm bar from the mount is to "ride" the push, giving your opponent the sensation that his push is effective while in reality you are just locking his arms in place and positioning yourself for the finish.

1 Greg is mounted on Peter. Peter extends his arms and pushes on Greg's chest in an attempt to remove him from the mount. Greg wants to "ride" the push and set up the arm bar so he leans forward with his chest pressing down on Peter's hands as if he is trying to fight the push. Greg decides to attack Peter's right arm, so as he leans forward Greg loops his left arm around Peter's right arm, placing the hand on his chest. Greg then slides his right arm between Peter's arms, placing his right hand on top of the left one. Greg shifts his weight to his left as he slides the left knee up towards Peter's head so his thigh is next to Peter's right arm, blocking him from pulling it back. Notice that Greg is still leaning forward pushing his weight against Peter's hands. This will force Peter to fight back while keeping his arms extended for the arm bar.

OPTIONAL TECHNIQUES

Mount-7, 10, 11, 26, 27, 28, 54, 65, 66, 86

ANATOMY OF TECHNIQUES

H) Elbow Separation

2 Greg puts most of his weight on his arms and Peter's arms as he leans forward and to his right. This makes it easy for him to raise his hips and lift the right leg up so he can plant the foot next to Peter's chest. Notice that as he leans to the right Greg's hips come in tight against Peter's arm so the arm-lock is tight. In one motion Greg circles the left leg around Peter's head until he lands his left foot on the mat on the left side of Peter's head. Greg drops his body down with his buttocks right next to Peter's shoulder. He extends Peter's arm as he leans back, lengthening his torso and driving his hips up against Peter's right elbow to hyperextend the joint. Notice that Greg keeps his feet parallel to each other and the knees tightly together.

INCORRECT

2 If Peter has both arms and elbows inside Greg's legs, Greg must keep his knees together. Otherwise Peter will be able to push the left leg off with his arms and get his head over the leg, escaping the submission attempt.

ALTERNATIVE

2 If Peter has both arms and elbows inside, Greg may choose to cross his feet so as to maintain a lock with his legs around Peter's arm, thus taking away Peter's ability to push the leg off and escape the arm-lock.

STRAIGHT ARM-BAR FROM THE GUARD

Being able to fight with your back on the ground is a huge asset in a combative situation. While traditional wisdom dictates that the person on the bottom is losing the battle, modern fighting techniques based on Gracie Jiu-Jitsu give the fighter the weapons not only to defend and protect himself when on the bottom but to actually finish a fight via submission. One of the most effective submissions from the guard is the arm-lock. With quick and proper execution you will surprise your assailant and submit him.

1 Greg has his back on the ground with Peter inside his guard. Peter has both hands around Greg's neck as he attempts to choke him. Greg grabs Peter's right elbow with his left hand as he moves his torso to his right and begins to slide his right hand in front of Peter's left leg.

a

b

c

2 Greg hooks his right arm behind Peter's left leg at the knee and uses it to pull his torso further to the right. At the same time, Greg places his left foot on Peter's right hip and pushes off it to help turn his body to the right and raise his hips up. Greg slides his right leg up towards Peter's head, locking the calf behind the left shoulder. Greg grabs Peter's right wrist with both hands. Greg presses down with the right calf on Peter's shoulder to help raise his hips up and lock them under Peter's right arm, trapping the elbow as he kicks the left leg up over the head. Greg brings the left leg down on Peter's head, forcing it down as he extends the hips up to press against Peter's right elbow. This hyperextends it for the arm-lock.

a

b

2 Notice Greg's use of his right forearm hooked behind Peter's left knee: it helps bring his torso around to the right, reaching the perfect angle for his legs to secure the arm-lock. Also notice Greg's right leg position as it rose up and locked behind Peter's right shoulder. Greg will press his right calf down on Peter's shoulder to help keep him from stepping out and escaping the arm-lock while at the same time helping Greg raise his hips and loop the left leg over Peter's head.

c

OPTIONAL TECHNIQUES

Guard-14, 15, 32, 33, 34, 35, 36, 37, 42, 43, 62, 63, 64, 65, 66, 67, 68, 69, 70

ANATOMY OF TECHNIQUES

H) Elbow Separation

SWEEP FROM THE ATTEMPTED STRAIGHT ARM-BAR

Many times as you attempt a straight arm-bar from the guard your opponent will lean forward, applying his weight down on your legs to try to prevent you from extending his arm for the arm-lock. This is a common and effective counter to the arm-lock. Any time this happens this sweep will be available and is the perfect counter to his defense.

1 As Greg loops his left leg around Peter's head to secure the arm-lock, Peter counters it by leaning forward and applying his weight down on Greg's legs, stacking them over the head.

2 Greg senses that his arm-lock attempt is foiled and also notices Peter's over-commitment, with his weight forward, to defend the arm-lock. Greg quickly switches to the sweep. While still controlling Peter's right arm, Greg swings his left leg back down to the left in a pendulum motion. He uses the momentum of the movement to help kick his right leg down and across Peter's side in a chopping motion which forces Peter to roll over his right shoulder. Greg helps the roll by using his right arm to push up Peter's left leg over. As Peter begins to roll over, Greg scissors the left leg under Peter.

3 As Peter's back hits the ground, Greg opens the left arm, plants the hand wide on the mat and pushes off it to help propel himself over the top of Peter. Greg ends up mounted on Peter. Notice that Greg's sweeping motion isn't to the side but rather over his left shoulder.

OPTIONAL TECHNIQUES
Guard-13, 15, 32, 33, 34, 35, 36, 37, 42, 43, 62, 63, 64, 65, 66, 67, 68, 69, 70

FOLLOW UP TECHNIQUES
Mount-7, 10, 11, 12, 26, 27, 28, 54, 65, 66, 86

SCISSORS SWEEP

Being able to sweep your opponent, switching your position from bottom to top is a formidable weapon to have in a fight. The scissors sweep is such a simple and effective sweep that it is a staple in the arsenal of most successful fighters. The key to any sweep is to be able to block your opponent's ability to brace to one side and then get him off balance to that side. To make the scissors sweep effective you need to bring your opponent's weight forward on top of your legs so you can easily reverse him with your legs' scissoring motion.

REVERSE

1 Greg has Peter in his guard. His right hand grabs behind Peter's left elbow and the left hand is inside the lapel to set up a choke. It is always preferable to have two attacking options at all times to divert your opponent's attention. In this case, Greg's hand in the collar calls Peter's attention to preventing the choke. As Peter steps up with his right leg in an attempt to stand, Greg opens his legs. He drops the right leg to the ground, bent at the knee, next to Peter's left leg to block it. Greg bends the left leg to insert the knee in front of Peter's hips so his left shin blocks the hips and supports Peter's weight as he attempts to push forward.

1 Notice Greg's left leg bent at the knee with his shin in front of Peter's hips blocking them and supporting their weight. Greg's left foot hooks on the outside of Peter's right hip and will help in the sweep by kicking the hip up and over.

2 Greg arches back with his torso as he pulls Peter's body on top of him with his hands. Peter's weight is now far forward with most of it resting on Greg's left shin, making Peter's legs very light. Greg scissors his legs as he pulls Peter's left arm in, forcing him to fall over.

OPTIONAL TECHNIQUES
Guard-13, 14, 15, 32, 33, 34, 35, 36, 37, 42, 43, 62, 63, 64, 65, 66, 67, 68, 69, 70

FOLLOW UP TECHNIQUES
Mount-7, 10, 11, 12, 26, 27, 28, 54, 65, 66, 86

3 Greg uses Peter's falling momentum to follow him, using his arms to pull him over the top.

CLOSE THE GAP AND ACHIEVE THE CLINCH

Since your fighting skills greatly involve ground fighting, being able to close the gap and clinch your opponent without being hit with a strong strike is a must. Keys to closing the gap are avoiding being at striking distance any longer than necessary and quickly and safely shooting in while protecting your face and body from your attacker's strikes.

1 Greg and Peter square off facing each other. Peter has his hands in striking position ready to throw punches. Greg's hands are open with the palms facing Peter, ready to intercept and block Peter's punches before they can do any damage.

2 Greg cuts the distance as he takes a forward step with his left leg, having started with his left leg forward. Greg keeps his arms and hands in front of his face, arms bent at approximately 75°. He aims his face and hands to hit Peter's chest. Any punch attempts by Peter will be blocked by Greg's forearms. When his hands get close to Peter's chest, Greg opens his arms and wraps his hands over Peter's arms. He grabs the triceps and his forearms and elbows block the biceps. Greg now controls Peter's arms, and Peter cannot pull them back or strike forward.

3 Greg drops his right arm under Peter's left arm as he takes a step forward with his right leg to the outside of Peter's left leg. This lets him reach around Peter's back with the right arm and grab Peter's right side. Greg secures the clinch by having his hips tight against Peter's left hip. Notice that Greg's feet are firmly planted in base on both sides of Peter's left leg. Greg's left hand firmly grips and pulls down on Peter's right arm to bring his torso forward and slightly off balance.

REVERSE **3** Notice Greg's right forearm as it circles around Peter's left arm to reach under it and around the back to grab Peter's right side.

a   b   c

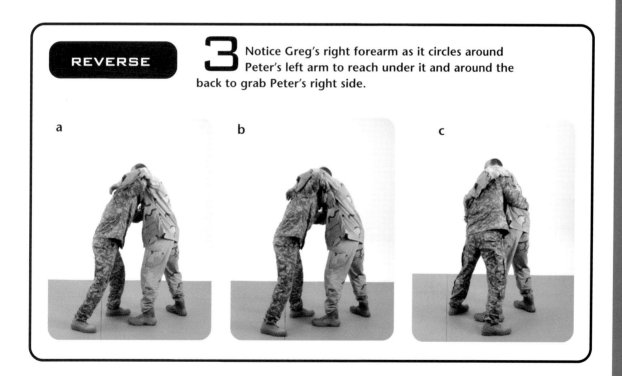

OPTIONAL TECHNIQUES

83, 84, 85

FOLLOW UP TECHNIQUES

Takedowns-17, 47, 51, 79, 80, 81, 87

FRONT TAKEDOWN TO THE MOUNT

After a successful clinch, the next step to victory is being able to take the fight to the ground and ending up on top in an advantageous position. With a resisting combatant, his reactions will generally dictate which technique you will use. One common reaction to being clinched is for the opponent to try to move away and break the clinch. In that case the front takedown works extremely well.

1 Greg clinches Peter. Greg could have a variety of other controlling grips such as the one in the previous technique: holding the hip and the elbow on opposite sides. As Peter tries to step away, Greg drops his body down so his head presses against Peter's chest and his hips move back. At the same time Greg bear hugs him over the right arm, locking his hands together behind Peter's back.

ALTERNATIVE

2 This move works the same way should Greg bear hug Peter under the arms. The key to breaking down the opponent's balance is to get low enough to cinch his lower back and then drive the head up on his chest, forcing it back.

2 Greg breaks Peter's balance by driving his head forward and pushing against Peter's chest while at the same time cinching his arm grip to pull Peter's waist in. This push and pull action causes Peter to start to fall backwards.

3 Greg controls Peter's fall by holding his body with his arms and steps over Peter's legs with the left leg. He ends up in the mounted position with Peter on the ground.

OPTIONAL TECHNIQUES

17, 47, 51, 79, 80, 81, 87

FOLLOW UP TECHNIQUES

Mount-7, 10, 11, 12, 26, 27, 28, 54, 65, 66, 86

REAR TAKEDOWN

Many times during the clinch and subsequent scramble that occurs, an opportunity may arise to get to your assailant's back and get a rear clinch. If there is a wall or a post nearby, try to maneuver him so you can drive the back of his head into the wall or post as he falls down. The rear clinch is a very good controlling position that you should take advantage of. A great option to take down the opponent from a rear clinch is shown here.

1 Greg has a rear clinch on Peter – his arms are cinched around Peter's waist and his feet are open slightly wider than shoulder width for base. Greg's face is pushing against Peter's right shoulder to protect it in case Peter throws a rear elbow strike with the right arm. Greg wants to take Peter down and end up in an advantageous position.

REVERSE

1 Notice Greg's handgrip: the fingers are interlocked.

INCORRECT

1 If Greg simply cups his hands over each other, Peter can pull and break one of his fingers.

2 Greg bends the left leg and drops his body down while extending the right leg so his foot touches Peter's right heel to block it. Greg's arms drop down to Peter's waist. Greg starts to sit down on his left heel, pulling Peter back in a clockwise circular motion with him. Since Peter cannot step back with his right leg, he loses his balance and falls to the ground. Notice that Greg does not fall back while pulling Peter on top of him but rather pulls Peter in a circular motion as if he wanted to sit past his own left foot. He turns Peter's body as he pulls him with his arms.

a
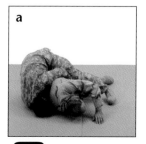

b
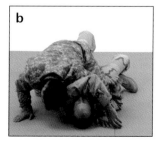

c
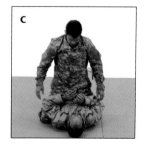

3 When they hit the ground, Greg uses the momentum of the fall to kick his left leg over Peter's legs and end up mounted on Peter.

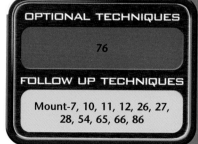

OPTIONAL TECHNIQUES

76

FOLLOW UP TECHNIQUES

Mount-7, 10, 11, 12, 26, 27, 28, 54, 65, 66, 86

FRONT GUILLOTINE CHOKE

A common takedown attempt in street fight and combat situations is the front tackle. The opponent charges forward with his arms open and head aimed at your torso to tackle and take you down. A great counter to the tackle is the front guillotine choke. Even if his tackle is successful and you end up on your back on the ground, once the guillotine is locked, you will still be able to choke out your opponent. The guillotine can also be applied from a standard clinch as it is demonstrated here.

Note: For weapon retention and transition you need to have your head on the weapon side (choke with left arm). To stop your opponent from transitioning to his weapon you need your head on his weapon side (choke with right arm).

a

1 Greg clinches Peter's head with both hands cupped behind the head pulling it down. Peter may attempt to drop down and tackle Greg. Peter's head is to the left of Greg's head.

b

c

2 Greg pulls Peter's head down with his hands until it is mid-torso and slides his left arm down along the right side of Peter's neck and his right arm along the left side.

REVERSE

2 Notice how Greg slides his hands, palm open and facing back against Peter's chest.

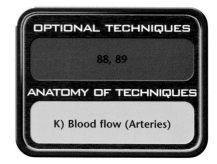

OPTIONAL TECHNIQUES

88, 89

ANATOMY OF TECHNIQUES

K) Blood flow (Arteries)

3 Greg wraps his left arm around Peter's neck so his forearm is under Peter's Adam's apple. Greg grabs his left wrist with his right hand forming a frame. Greg leans back and pulls his left forearm up with the right hand, pushing against Peter's throat to choke him. The direction of the forearm pull is up into the throat and not against the chin. It is very important for Greg to cinch the noose around Peter's neck before he applies the upwards choking pressure otherwise Peter's head may slip out of the guillotine.

DETAIL

3 This is a close up of the frame that Greg creates for the guillotine choke. His right hand cups under his left wrist with all five fingers together like a claw. Notice how Greg grabs his fingers over his left thumb so it can't be pulled back.

MODERN ARMY COMBATIVES

LEVEL II

Modern Combatives II adds more advanced moves to your hand-to-hand fighting repertoire. MAC II expands your horizons by teaching more techniques and greater options for a soldier. By learning and practicing the moves in Modern Army Combatives II you will have an increased mental imprint and understanding of the skill, techniques and strategies to be a better combative fighter.

DEFENSE AGAINST ATTEMPTS TO MOUNT: *Arch or bridge*

It is always best to prevent your opponent's advance rather than reacting later to escape the better position that he achieved. This is especially true in an attempt to mount you. This common and effective counter to the mount is based on sensitivity of his weight change, his body motion that sets up the mount, and timing.

1 Peter has side control on Greg, his hips facing up with his left leg forward and his right leg back. Peter grabs Greg's left leg with his right hand and starts to pull it across his body setting up the mount. Greg senses the attempt. Greg has good defensive posture with his right hand grabbing Peter's belt and his left arm under Peter's armpit.

2 As soon as he feels Peter's leg coming over the top in his motion to mount, Greg reacts by pushing off his feet and bridging to his right as he reaches up with his left hand as if he were trying to grab an object behind Peter. Greg's left arm pushing under Peter's armpit forces him back. Peter doesn't have a way to stop the reversal because his leg is up in the air. He ends up on his back with Greg now in side control.

a

b

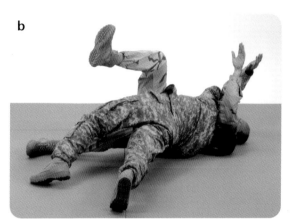

c

2 Notice how Greg drives his left arm under Peter's right armpit forcing him back. Also notice Greg's legwork. Immediately after he bridges, Greg continues to push off his left leg for power. Greg brings his right leg under the hips, planting the toes back on the mat to his right and pushes off it to help propel Peter backwards.

OPTIONAL TECHNIQUES

21, 60, 61

DEFENSE AGAINST ATTEMPTS TO MOUNT: *Back door escape*

Another very good and effective escape to the mount attempt is to escape by the back door. In this case, your opponent was successful at achieving the mount because you were either unsuccessful at bumping him because your timing was off or he may have surprised you with his attempt and you didn't react in time. Some fighters get so good at the backdoor escape that they actually prefer to let the opponent mount and use it.

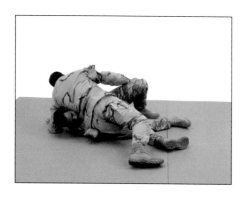

1 Peter has side control on Greg. His hips face up with his left leg forward and his right leg back. Peter grabs Greg's left leg with his right hand and starts to pull it across his body setting up the mount and Greg senses it. Greg has good defensive posture with his right arm bent at the elbow and the forearm under Peter's hips with the hand sticking out the other side. Greg's left arm is under Peter's armpit. In the backdoor escape Greg's right arm will do a lot of the work so it is important that it is properly positioned with the forearm against Peter's left hip. Greg's right leg is flat on the mat and bent in with the knee touching Peter's thigh.

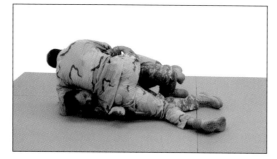 

2 Peter loops his right leg over Greg and mounts him. Greg coils his body, his right elbow touching his right thigh. As soon as Peter's right foot touches the ground, Greg pushes off his left foot and moves his body under Peter who, at this point, has not fully established the mount and is very light. Pivoting off his elbow, Greg drives his right forearm towards his left, pushing Peter's hip in that same direction. Greg's right knee slides under Peter's left leg at the same time. Notice how Greg's right elbow touching the top of the thigh forms a block to prevent Peter's left leg from touching the ground. Greg loops his right arm around Peter, locking the hand on his right side to help pull himself to the back.

REVERSE **2** Notice how Greg's left arm keeps Peter off balance even as he is mounted. Also Greg's head, under Peter's left armpit, blocks Peter's left arm from coming around in front of Greg's head and is in a perfect position to push the upper body towards his left, helping him take Peter's back.

3 Greg continues to push off his left foot and move to his right as he gets to Peter's back.

4 Should Peter manage to bring his left arm around Greg's head or if he defends Greg from taking his back by pushing his weight to his left, Greg simply pushes off his right foot, slides his left knee in front of Peter's hips and moves his body back under Peter's body, replacing the guard.

a

b
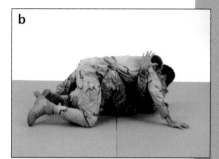

c

d

e

ALTERNATIVE

Many fighters prefer to grab the opponent's pants at the knee and simply lift it up and over the leg as they go for the backdoor escape. This will not work if the opponent is not wearing long pants so master both techniques.

a

b

c

d

OPTIONAL TECHNIQUES

20, 60, 61

57

ESCAPE THE HALF GUARD

Often when fighting you will find yourself stuck in your opponent's half-guard. If you are not adept at escaping the half-guard, you may be forced into your opponent's closed guard, or worse, fall for a reversal or a submission. Therefore it is very important to know at least one solid way to escape and advance from the half-guard.

1 Greg is in Peter's half-guard with his right leg trapped between Peter's legs. Peter has good defensive posture with his left arm under Greg's right armpit. Peter wants to be on his side and not flat on his back to take advantage of the mobility that the half-guard offers, therefore Greg wants to deny him that position. Greg extends his left leg back and pushes off his left foot, driving his chest forward and pressing Peter's back flat on the ground.

2 Greg braces his right hand on Peter's left knee. He locks it in place as he walks his right foot forward, driving his right knee up until his knee escapes from between Peter's legs.

OPTIONAL TECHNIQUES

10, 11, 26, 27, 28, 31, 65, 66

FOLLOW UP TECHNIQUES

Mount-7, 10, 11, 12, 26, 27, 28, 54, 65, 66, 86

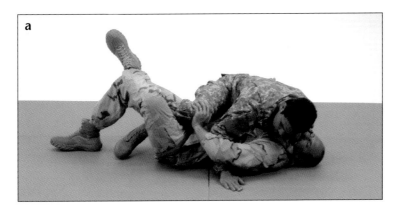

3 Peter senses he is losing the control of the position and uses his left hand to block Greg's right knee from advancing any further forward. Greg slides his right arm under Peter's left arm and plants the hand on the ground. Greg climbs his right hand up by cupping the ground and doing a "caterpillar crawl." This means that he cups the hand, bringing the back of the palm forward and then reaching out with the fingers for a new grip, repeating this as a way to move the hand forward while maintaining contact between his hand and the ground. As Greg's hand moves up towards Peter's head, his right arm pushes up against Peter's left arm, raising it up and removing the block on his knee. Greg continues to drive his right knee forward using his body weight and his upward pressure to finally release his right foot from between Peter's legs, achieving the mounted position.

ESCAPE THE HEAD-LOCK: *Form the frame*

Being stuck in a head-lock on the ground is a demoralizing and uncomfortable position to be in. Having control of your head, your opponent not only can apply pressure to your head with his arms and body but can also deliver short punches and knees to your face. Here Greg demonstrates one escape from the head-lock – the frame. The frame is effective when your opponent has his head away from you when applying a headlock.

1 Peter has Greg in a headlock on the ground with his right arm wrapped around the head. The first thing Greg needs to do to escape the head-lock is to turn on his side and not lie flat with his back on the ground. Greg immediately turns to his right side, placing his right elbow on the ground and tucking his chin in. Since Peter's head is away from Greg's head, Greg will use the frame escape. He places his left forearm in front of Peter's face and grabs his left hand with his right hand forming a frame. This frame will keep Peter from applying any additional pressure on Greg's head with his head-lock. Notice the frame. Greg's right elbow is on the ground with the forearm up. His right hand locks onto his left hand with the forearm braced against Peter's right side of the jaw. Anytime Peter tries to lean forward and apply his body weight on Greg, the pressure gets transferred down to the ground via the frame. Also Greg's forearm pressing against Peter's jaw/throat area is very uncomfortable for Peter.

2 Greg opens his left leg out to the left and steps back with his foot, pushing off it to drive his body in a counter-clockwise direction. Since Peter's face is still pressed by Greg's frame, and because he can't lean against Greg's torso, Peter is forced to lean back.

3 Once he is in a straight line with Peter, Greg loops his left leg over Peter's head, pushing it down and further forcing Peter on his back. Greg continues his circling motion, ending up on top of Peter while still in a head-lock.

a

b

c

d

REVERSE

3 Notice Greg's left leg catching the front of Peter's face and pressing it down, forcing him to further fall on his back.

a

b

c

4 Reversing the angle for best viewing: Greg opens his arms wide, planting his hands in front of Peter to prevent him from rolling to his left and pulling down on Greg's head to roll him over. Greg places his right hand on Peter's left leg, pinning it to the ground, and loops his right leg over Peter's body. His foot lands tightly against Peter's waist, taking away any space for him to try to escape.

a

b

c

5 Again, Greg opens his arm out and plants his hands to protect from being rolled. Greg brings his left knee up, getting it as close to Peter's head as he can. He then leans back and sits on his left heel so his weight is back, making it very difficult for Peter to roll him to the left. To break Peter's head-lock, Greg makes a frame with his arms, his left forearm pressing down on Peter's right side of the jaw, his right hand grabbing over the left hand, forming a square frame with his arms. Greg leans to his left, putting his weight on the frame and pressing the forearm against Peter's head, forcing him to release the grip. Notice that Greg does not try to break the grip by pulling his head up, as this would create a lot of stress on his neck and would most likely not work against a strong and determined opponent. Instead he leans towards his left elbow, applying his body weight on the frame and transferring it to the forearm. The pressure of the forearm against Peter's head is excruciating and he will be forced to release the grip.

OPTIONAL TECHNIQUES

24, 25

FOLLOW UP TECHNIQUES

7, 29, 28

H2H
TECHNIQUE 024
MODERN ARMY COMBATIVES LEVEL II

ESCAPE THE HEADLOCK:
Follow the leg

Another common headlock situation is for your opponent to have his head close to yours, making it impossible to use the frame escape. In that case, you need to use the follow the leg escape.

1 Peter has Greg in a headlock. Peter has his head close to Greg's, making it impossible for Greg to use the frame escape. Greg will use the following leg escape. Greg has good defensive posture. Since he's on his right side, he reaches with his left hand and grabs Peter's left shoulder. Greg steps out with his left leg and rotates his body back in a counter-clockwise direction, using the left hand to pull Peter by the shoulder.

2 If Peter doesn't react by leaning forward, Greg will simply roll him backwards. As Peter reacts, Greg loops his left leg over Peter's left leg, locking his heel on Peter's thigh.

3 Taking further advantage of Peter's lean, Greg extends his right leg and pushes off the right foot and hand, using his shoulder to force Peter flat on his face. Although he is flat on his stomach, Peter has not released the headlock on Greg yet.

4 Reversing the angle for viewing: Greg opens his right arm out, planting the right hand wide for base to keep Peter from rolling him back over. Greg pushes off his hand and feet and jumps over to Peter's left side. He then drives his body forward, pressing his left shoulder down against Peter's shoulders. The pressure on Peter is very strong and most fighters will release the headlock right there.

5 Should Peter be very stubborn and continue to maintain the headlock, Greg uses his right hand on Peter's right wrist to pull and break the grip. He then pulls up on the wrist while still keeping it wrapped over his head, pivoting it around the shoulder and applying torque to the joint for the submission.

OPTIONAL TECHNIQUES

23, 25

FOLLOW UP TECHNIQUES

Rear mount-9, 30, 65, 66

ESCAPE THE HEADLOCK: *Arch over*

Another common way for an attacker to grip you in a headlock is for the attacker to pull up on your elbow while pushing off his feet and pressing his body back against your body. In that case the arch over is the proper defensive choice. The key to this escape is the direction of the arch: straight over the shoulder and not to the side.

1 Peter has Greg in a headlock. Peter pulls Greg's right elbow up with his left hand and pushes off his feet to press his torso against Greg's body to pin him. Greg is in good defensive position turned to his right side. Greg wraps his arms tightly around Peter's chest as high as possible, locking his hands together with the palms facing each other. Greg steps out with his left leg and rotates his body in a counterclockwise direction until he is near 90° with Peter's body.

a

b

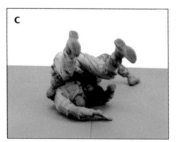

c

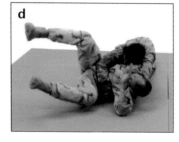

d

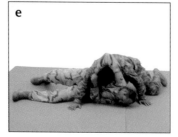

e

2 Greg pushes off his feet and legs, arching over his right shoulder. Notice, that as he arches, Greg also cinches the arm grip around Peter's chest, pulling him up. This entire movement forces Peter's body forward. Peter has to release the headlock and use his left hand to brace, otherwise he will be turned over. At this point, Peter's weight is no longer on top of Greg but rather concentrated on his left arm and head. Greg continues to push off his legs and rotates on his shoulders while still pulling Peter with his arms. This forces Peter to roll forward and over his head. Notice that Greg's intention is to drive Peter's head to the mat with great force. Once he achieves that he has Peter's weight on his head, making it easy for him to roll him over. Greg ends up on top of Peter.

OPTIONAL TECHNIQUES

23, 24

FOLLOW UP TECHNIQUES

Side mount-4, 5, 10, 11, 26, 28, 31, 46, 54, 65, 66, 86

PAPER CUTTER CHOKE

The paper cutter choke is a surprisingly effective choke from the mount. Because of its quick and simple execution this choke is a favorite of many fighters. The key to this choke is to use your body weight to apply pressure on the opponent's neck. This choke can also be done from side control and half-guard.

1 Greg is mounted on Peter. Greg grabs Peter's right lapel with his left hand and opens it up. This allows his right hand to reach inside with the thumb and grip the collar as deep as possible.

DETAIL

2 Greg quickly drives his right elbow down and grabs the left lapel with his left hand. Greg continues to drive his right elbow towards the ground, using his weight on the elbow to drive his forearm against Peter's throat. At the same time he pulls on Peter's right collar with the left hand, tightening the noose for the choke.

DETAIL

2 The proper forearm position for the choke is with the blade of the forearm pressing down against the opponent's throat for maximum pressure.

OPTIONAL TECHNIQUES

Side mount 4, 5, 11, 28, 31, 46, 54, 65, 66
Mount-7, 10, 11, 12, 27, 28, 54, 65, 66, 86
half guard-10, 11, 22, 27, 28, 31, 65, 66

NUTCRACKER CHOKE

Another very quick and effective choke from the mount is the nutcracker choke. Again the key with this choke, much like the paper cutter choke, is the use of the body weight to apply extra choking pressure. This choke can also be done from side control and half-guard.

1 Greg is mounted on Peter. Peter's hands are low, pushing against Greg's hips as he tries to escape the mount.

2 Greg quickly grabs Peter's collar with his hands. Notice that Greg grabs the collar with the same side hand (not crossing over), his fingers inside and the thumb out as close to Peter's neck as possible for best pressure. Greg turns his hands in so his knuckles press against Peter's throat and leans forward with his body using his weight to add pressure to the choke.

OPTIONAL TECHNIQUES

Mount-7, 10, 11, 12, 26, 28, 54, 65, 66, 86 In half guard-10, 11, 22, 26, 28, 31, 65, 66

LEANING CHOKE

A variation of the nutcracker choke is the leaning choke. In this case, Greg will cross his hands in front of Peter's throat using a push-pull action and his body weight to apply the choking pressure. This choke may be easier to apply than the nutcracker choke as you don't have to grip the collar as tightly to be successful.

1 Greg is mounted on Peter. Peter has his hands low and is not protecting his neck. Greg grabs the collar with the same side hand (not crossing over), his fingers inside and the thumb out. Notice that Greg doesn't grab the collar very tight, he needs a little space to execute the next step.

2 Greg twists his shoulders to his right, driving his left hand down and across Peter's throat and using the right collar to choke Peter. Greg leans forward using his body weight to add further pressure to his left hand as it pushes down to the mat while pulling up the left collar with his right hand.

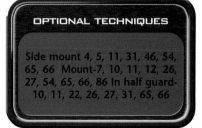

OPTIONAL TECHNIQUES

Side mount 4, 5, 11, 31, 46, 54, 65, 66 Mount-7, 10, 11, 12, 26, 27, 54, 65, 66, 86 In half guard- 10, 11, 22, 26, 27, 31, 65, 66

COLLAR CHOKE

The collar choke is one of the basic and most effective chokes when you have your opponent's back. By using his collar to cut out the blood flow to the brain, this choke will work against even the most stubborn and determined adversary.

1 Greg has back control on Peter. Greg's feet hooked in front of Peter's hips keep him from moving from side to side to escape the control. Greg slides the right arm under Peter's right arm. With his right hand Greg grabs and opens Peter's right collar making it easy for the left hand to secure a deep grip on the collar.

2 Greg reaches around Peter's neck with his left arm and grabs the right collar as high and tight around the neck as possible. Notice how Greg's right hand pulls down on Peter's collar making it tight so his left hand can slide up the collar for a tight grip. Greg grips the collar with the thumb inside and the fingers outside.

3 Having secured the important grip with his left hand, Greg grabs the left collar with his right hand. Notice that in order to have the best leverage to execute the choke, Greg has the choking arm (left arm) over Peter's arm and the tightening arm (right arm) under Peter's arm.

4 Greg applies the choking pressure by twisting his shoulders counter-clockwise with his left hand pulling Peter's right collar across his neck and the right hand pulling Peter's left collar down to tighten the noose around the neck.

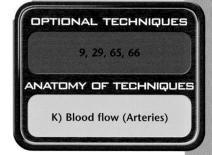

OPTIONAL TECHNIQUES

9, 29, 65, 66

ANATOMY OF TECHNIQUES

K) Blood flow (Arteries)

SINGLE WING CHOKE

A great variation of the collar choke is the single wing choke. Instead of using the opposite collar pull down for choking leverage, Greg uses his hand wrapped around Peter's arm to press the back of the head. This choke may be easier to apply at those times when you have a tough time grabbing the second collar due to your opponent's struggles.

1 Greg has back control on Peter. Greg's feet hooked in front of Peter's hips keep him from moving from side to side to escape the control. Greg slides the right arm under Peter's right arm. With his right hand, Greg grabs and opens Peter's right collar, making it easy for the left hand to secure a deep grip on the collar.

2 Greg reaches up with his right arm, circling it around Peter's right arm and aims the hand towards the back of Peter's neck.

3 Greg applies the choking pressure by sliding and turning his body to his right while his left hand pulls Peter's right collar tight against his throat. Greg adds pressure to the choke by sliding the right forearm across the back of Peter's neck, forcing it forward and creating the proper choking leverage to cut off the blood flow. Notice that Greg slides his right hand with the palm facing back.

ANATOMY OF TECHNIQUES

K) Blood flow (Arteries)

REVERSE BENT ARM BAR FROM SIDE CONTROL

Side control is a very good position to be in during a fight. With your body weight pressing and controlling your opponent's body and your legs and feet free to move and adjust to his attempts to escape, the side control is perhaps the preferred position to be in for stability and to apply submissions. The reverse bent arm-bar is usually available when in side control and is a great fight ender and effective at stopping your opponent from transitioning to a weapon.

a

b

c

1 Greg has side control on Peter. His body is at a 90° angle with Peter's and his chest presses down on Peter's chest to pin him to the mat. Peter has good defensive position with his left arm under Greg's right armpit. As Peter attempts to escape by moving his body to his left, Greg adjusts his position, turning his hips and shoulders in a clockwise direction. This exposes Peter's arm for the submission. Greg reaches with his right hand, sliding it up Peter's forearm until he can grip the wrist.

a

2 Greg twists his body back to the original side control position, using his torso movement to force Peter's arm down to the mat. Greg wraps the left arm under and around Peter's left arm until he can grab his right wrist with his own left hand, securing a lock on Peter's arm.

b

c

3 Greg continues moving his legs so his hips are facing towards Peter's head. His right leg goes forward while his left loops back with the toes pushing the ground. Pushing off his right foot, Greg loops his left leg over Peter's head, landing the foot next to it. Pushing off his left foot, Greg leans back as he uses his arms and torso to turn Peter's left arm around the shoulder, applying torque to the joint for the submission.

OPTIONAL TECHNIQUES

Side mount-4, 5, 10, 11, 26, 28, 46, 54, 65, 66, 86

ANATOMY OF TECHNIQUES

F) Kimura Separation

TRIANGLE CHOKE

The triangle choke is another basic and effective choke in combative fighting. By using your legs and one of your opponent's arms to apply the choking pressure, the triangle choke is effective whether you are fighting in fatigues or not. The main requirement of the triangle choke is for your opponent to have one arm outside of your legs. It is very common for an attacker to underhook your leg during a fight, it may be that he is attempting to pass your guard or during a scramble his arm may end up there somehow, creating opportunities to apply the triangle choke.

1 Peter's right arm underhooks Greg's left leg in his attempt to pass the guard. Greg controls Peter's left elbow with his right hand and uses his left hand to pull down on Peter's back of the head. For the triangle to be effective, it is very important for Greg to force Peter's head down and forward. Otherwise Peter can lean back and gain defensive posture, making it hard for Greg to properly wrap his legs around Peter's head and arm for the choke.

2 Greg places his right foot on Peter's left hip and pushes off it, escaping his hips to the right and turning his upper body to the left. Greg loops his left leg over Peter's back of the neck and bends the leg down, pressing the back of his calf down against Peter's head to prevent him from moving away. Notice that Greg is still controlling Peter's left arm with his right hand to prevent him from pulling it out and negating the triangle.

3 Greg switches to his left hand to control Peter's left arm and grabs his left ankle with his right hand, securing the lock with his leg around Peter's head and left arm. Notice how Greg pulls down on his ankle, forcing the calf to press down against Peter's head.

4 Greg loops his right leg over the left, locking the back of his right knee over the left ankle and completing the triangle lock around Peter's head and left arm. Greg applies the choking pressure by bringing his knees together and towards his chest while at the same time using both hands to pull down on Greg's head. The choking pressure is created by Greg's left thigh against the right side of Peter's throat and Peter's own left arm pressing against the right side of his throat.

Triangle variation

Another way to achieve the triangle is to force your opponent to have one of his arms under your leg, as in this case.

1 This time, instead of waiting for Peter to make the mistake, Greg initiates it himself. He places both feet on the hips and extends the legs, pushing Peter away while controlling both wrists with his hands. This creates space in front of Peter's arms for Greg to curl and slide his left leg up between Peter's arms.

2 The mechanics now are similar to the previous triangle set up. Greg pushes off his right foot, turning his shoulders to the left while opening up Peter's right arm with his left hand. Greg loops the right leg over the left ankle, locking the triangle. Greg applies the choking pressure the same way as in the previous version: bringing his knees together and towards his chest while at the same time using both hands to pull down on Greg's head.

OPTIONAL TECHNIQUES

Guard-13, 14, 15, 32, 33, 34, 35, 36, 37, 42, 43, 62, 63, 64, 65, 66, 67, 68, 69, 70

ELEVATOR SWEEP #1

Although you have the tools to fight from the bottom, most everyone prefers to fight from the top. Being able to reverse position from being on the bottom to being on the top is a great asset to have in a physical battle. The elevator sweep takes advantage of your opponent's attempt to pass the guard as he raises one leg to gain some leverage advantage.

1 Peter has his right leg up as he attempts to pass Greg's guard. Greg turns to his right, dropping the right knee down slightly as he escapes his hips to the left. Greg escapes his hips further out to his left as he drops the right leg to the mat and bends the left leg down and loops the foot around Peter's right leg to lock it under Peter's right thigh. Greg grabs the back of Peter's collar with his left hand while his right hand grabs the back of Peter's left elbow.

74

2 In one move, Greg uses his left hand on Peter's collar to pull him forward. At the same time, Greg uses his right hand to pull Peter's left elbow and his left foot to pull Peter's right thigh. This forces Peter off balance with his weight falling forward and on top of Greg. Greg scissors the right leg, kicking Peter's left leg from under him. At the same time, Greg kicks his left leg up and to the right, elevating Peter's right leg over to the right as well, forcing him to fall to his back while Greg ends up mounted on him.

REVERSE **2** Notice how Greg uses his left foot to lift and drive Peter's right leg over while he hooks his right foot on Peter's left leg. At the same time, he scissors the right leg in, taking Peter's left leg from under him and causing the reversal.

OPTIONAL TECHNIQUES

Guard-32, 34

FOLLOW UP TECHNIQUES

Mount-7, 10, 11, 12, 26, 27, 28, 54, 65, 66, 86

ELEVATOR SWEEP #2

Another great way to apply the elevator sweep is when your adversary tries to choke you from the mount. In this case, Greg not only demonstrates the elbow escape from the mount but the use of the elevator sweep as a counter to the choke.

1 Peter is mounted on Greg and applying a hand choke by pressing his right hand on Greg's throat. Greg uses his hands to release the pressure and set up the escape and the sweep. His right hand grabs and pushes Peter's right wrist while his left hand grabs the back of Peter's elbow. Greg tries the bridge escape but Peter opens his right leg out to brace and stop the roll. Greg immediately changes to the elbow escape – he coils his left leg in, bringing the left knee under Peter's right leg.

2 Greg escapes his hips to the left while placing his stiff right arm on Peter's left hip. Greg loops his left leg around Peter's right leg while at the same time he coils his right leg, bringing his knee under Peter's left thigh while leaving his right foot underhooking it. Greg slides his left arm under Peter's right armpit, wrapping it around the arm until his hand touches the top of his head. Greg escapes his hips back to the right.

REVERSE

2 Notice Greg's leg and hip work. As Greg's hips move from his left to right, his feet get in position; the right leg with the foot underhooking Peter's left thigh is the elevator and the left leg drops to the ground to act as the scissor to clear Peter's right knee brace on the mat.

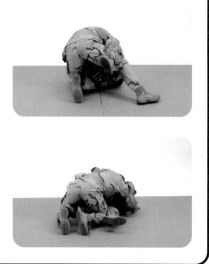

OPTIONAL TECHNIQUES

Guard-13, 14, 15, 32, 33, 35, 36, 37, 42, 43, 62, 63, 64, 65, 66, 67, 68, 69, 70

FOLLOW UP TECHNIQUES

Mount-7, 10, 11, 12, 26, 27, 28, 54, 65, 66, 86

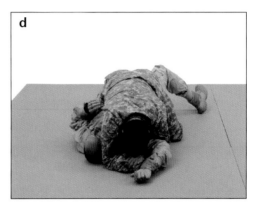

3 Greg continues to escape his hips to the right and initiates the sweep by kicking and scissoring his legs. Greg kicks the right foot up, sending Peter's left leg over while he scissors his left leg in, clearing Peter's right knee from the mat for the reversal. Greg's left arm traps Peter's right arm and prevents him from using it to stop the motion. Greg ends up mounted on Peter and can go for a bent arm lock on Peter's right arm.

REVERSE **3** Notice that Greg's legs act in unison, the right leg kicks up while the left one scissors in, causing Peter to rotate and fall to his back.

REVERSE BENT ARM-BAR FROM THE GUARD

Having multiple attack options from any position is a great advantage to have during combat. The ability to switch between them will distract your adversary from one front to various fronts, confusing him and forcing him to select which attack to defend. Another great submission from the guard is the reverse bent arm-bar. This attack works any time your opponent's arm is next to his body and not grabbing anything, or for stopping your opponent from transitioning to a weapon or using one. Here Greg demonstrates the most common situation: when the opponent has his arm down with the hand on the mat.

1 Greg has Peter in his guard. Peter has his arms next to Greg's body with the hands on the ground. He may be using them to brace and regain his balance or to push off and stand up. Greg sees the opportunity for the reverse bent arm-bar, so he grabs Peter's left wrist with his right hand, four fingers on one side and the thumb on the other. Greg opens his legs and plants the right foot on the ground, pushing off it to escape his hips back and to the left.

2 Greg sits up, turning his shoulders to the right and pivoting off his right elbow so he can lasso his left arm around Peter's left arm (over the triceps area). Greg grabs his right wrist with the left hand, securing the lock around Peter's left arm. It is very important that his left arm is above Peter's elbow as he wraps it otherwise the lock won't work. Also notice how Greg secures the lock with his left hand grabbing the right wrist.

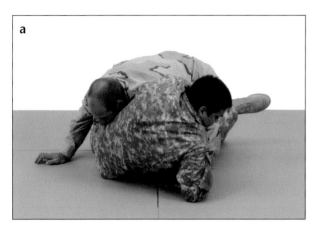

3 Greg drops his back to the ground as he twists his body counterclockwise. He uses the power of the movement to turn Peter's arm around the shoulder. Greg continues to move his torso to the right as he loops his right leg over Peter's back to prevent him from rolling forward and defending the submission. Greg re-locks his feet around Peter and continues to torque the arm around the shoulder for the submission. Notice that Greg uses his body movement to drive Peter's arm around instead of trying to muscle it with his arms alone. This is very important, especially if you are fighting against a stronger opponent.

OPTIONAL TECHNIQUES

Guard-13, 14, 15, 32, 33, 34, 36, 37, 42, 43, 62, 63, 64, 65, 66, 67, 68, 69, 70

ANATOMY OF TECHNIQUES

F) Kimura Separation

TIMING SWEEP: *Hip heist*

At times your opponent leans back so much that he opens himself up for the hip heist sweep. Most of the time this is a timing sweep, taking advantage of your opponent's over-commitment to leaning back, but it can also be used in conjunction with the reverse bent arm-bar. If your opponent leans back to defend the reverse attempt then the sweep is the proper option; if he leans forward to counter the sweep, the reverse bent arm-bar will apply.

1 Greg has Peter in his closed guard. Peter is leaning back with his arms at his side and the hands touching the ground.

2 Greg takes advantage of Peter's lean and opens his legs, dropping the right leg to the mat as he sits up. He twists his shoulders to the right and reaches with the left arm around Peter's left arm, grabbing the back of the elbow.

3 Greg pushes off his feet and continues the twisting motion with his body. As he drives his hips against Peter's hips he forces Peter to fall to his left. Notice that Greg pulls Peter's left arm in removing it from blocking the reversal. Greg ends up mounted on Peter and opens his arms out, placing the hands on the mat for balance and to prevent Peter from rolling him back over.

OPTIONAL TECHNIQUES

Guard-13, 14, 15, 32, 33, 34, 35, 37, 42, 43, 62, 63, 64, 65, 66, 67, 68, 69, 70

FOLLOW UP TECHNIQUES

Mount-7, 10, 11, 12, 26, 27, 28, 54, 65, 66, 86

GUILLOTINE CHOKE
FROM THE GUARD

The third attack of this combination is the guillotine from the guard. Your adversary may try to defend the hip heist sweep by leaning forward and arching his head; if he does so, he becomes vulnerable to the guillotine. The sequence of attacks is interchangeable depending on the opponent's reaction – the reverse bent arm-bar, the hip heist and the guillotine. Always have your head on your weapon side when applying the guillotine.

1 Greg has Peter in his closed guard. Greg sees Peter's hands on the ground with the arms next to his body in a perfect position for the reverse bent arm-bar, so he attempts it. Peter reacts and counters by leaning back, so Greg switches for the hip heist sweep. Once again, Peter counters properly by straightening his back and arching his head back, exposing his neck for the guillotine. Greg reaches over the back of Peter's neck and wraps his left arm around it.

REVERSE

1 Notice how Greg props himself off his right arm to sit up and slide his hips back, allowing space for his left arm to encircle Peter's neck.

2 Greg pushes off his right arm and scoots his hips back to allow space for his left arm to completely encircle Peter's neck and his left hand to come clear out the right side. Notice that Greg's palm is facing back towards his chest. Greg reaches with his right hand, grabs his own left wrist and cinches the noose around Peter's neck by bringing the left forearm up and left elbow in tight against it.

3 Having cinched the choke, Greg wraps his legs around Peter's back and leans back until his back touches the ground. He then applies the guillotine choke by using the right hand to pull the left forearm up against Peter's throat while at the same time extending his legs to drive Peter's body away, adding pressure to the choke. It is extremely important for Greg to cinch his arm around Peter's neck before he leans back, otherwise Peter's head may pop out of the choke as Greg extends his legs to push Peter's body back.

OPTIONAL TECHNIQUES

Guard-13, 14, 15, 32, 33, 34, 35, 36, 42, 43, 62, 63, 64, 65, 66, 67, 68, 69, 70

PASSING THE GUARD WITH THE KNEE ON THE TAILBONE

Having multiple options for every position is very important in a fight. Not only can you confuse your adversary with multiple attacks and options but often one technique will fit your style better than others in certain situations. The knee on the tailbone guard pass is a solid and effective guard pass against anyone, especially bigger opponents.

a

b

c

1 Greg is inside Peter's closed guard. His hands grip Peter's belt or top of the pants firmly, his elbows are close to his body and inside Peter's thighs, and his knees are closed in tight against Peter's hips taking away his mobility. Greg brings his left knee in to the center of Peter's hips, placing it right behind the tailbone. He then steps out with his right leg, planting the right foot wide and slightly back. Greg leans back, using the weight of his body to force Peter to open his legs and breaking the closed guard. Notice that while his left knee presses against Peter's tailbone to keep the hips locked in position, Greg's back pushes against Peter's calves, forcing Peter to break open the legs.

a

b

c

2 Greg slides his right arm down in front of Peter's left thigh and plants the hand on the ground about a foot away from Peter's right hip. At this point, Greg must have his left elbow back and inside Peter's hips, otherwise he will be vulnerable to a triangle choke. Greg drops his right shoulder under Peter's left thigh and pushes off his right leg to raise his body. At the same time Greg grabs Peter's belt with the right hand. Notice that Greg's right arm is now wrapped around the outside of Peter's left leg. Also notice that Greg did not lift Peter's leg with his right arm but rather used his shoulder under the thigh and the push of his right leg to raise his body up to lift it. This is extremely important as most opponents will put weight on their legs to counter the lift. Greg's arm alone does not have enough power to lift Peter's leg!

3 Greg brings his left arm back, grabbing under Peter's pants with his left hand to prevent him from rolling over his head as Greg continues to push off his legs. Greg drives his shoulder against Peter's thigh as he reaches with his right hand and grabs Peter's right collar. With his grip solid on the collar, Greg changes his upwards push to a forward push against Peter's legs by extending the left leg while bending the right one. He pulls his torso towards Peter's chest using his right hand to pull the collar and stacking Peter's legs over his head. Greg steps around to the right with his right leg and uses his shoulder to push Peter's legs away and reach side control.

REVERSE **3** Notice how Greg changes the direction of his push from upwards to forward as he pulls himself down with his right hand, stacking Peter's legs over his head. Greg then steps around to the right and extends his body, using his shoulder to push and clear Peter's legs to the side.

OPTIONAL TECHNIQUES

Passing the Guard-3, 39, 40, 41, 44, 45, 58, 71

FOLLOW UP TECHNIQUES

Side Mount-4, 5, 10, 11, 26, 28, 31, 46, 54, 65, 66, 86

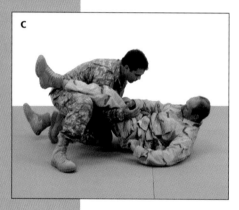

PASSING THE GUARD WITH THE KNEE ON THE TAILBONE: *Under both legs*

A variation of the knee on the tailbone is presented here, the under both legs pass. This variation has two major advantages over the previous one: it doesn't expose the passer to the triangle because both his arms are under the defender's legs and it also allows two ways to pass as you can pass to either side. Its biggest disadvantage is that it requires more power to raise both the opponent's legs and hips off the ground instead of just one leg as in the previous technique. You may find it harder to execute against bigger adversaries.

1 Greg uses the same principle as in the previous technique to break open Peter's legs. He places his left knee behind the tailbone, steps out with the right leg and leans back, using his back to force Peter's legs to open. This time however, Greg underhooks both of Peter's legs with his arms.

2 Greg drops both knees to the ground and extends his body in an explosive motion upwards and forward, thrusting Peter's legs up with his arms. At the height of the movement, Greg quickly dips his shoulder and knees down, allowing his shoulders to get under Peter's thighs and his arms to grab around Peter's legs. Greg locks his hands together. At this point, Greg can pass the guard to either side.

REVERSE

2 Notice how Greg grabs Peter's thighs with his hands, arms underhooking the thighs. He then drops his body down and gets his shoulders under the thighs so he can lock his hands together with the arms wrapped around Peter's legs.

3 Greg chooses to pass to his left. He reaches with his left hand and grabs Peter's left collar and uses his right hand to grab under Peter's pants as he pushes off his right leg. He drops his left knee forward, close to Peter's right shoulder. Greg stacks Peter's legs over his head and walks around to the left, using his shoulders to clear Peter's legs away and reach side control.

REVERSE **3** Greg uses his left arm to pull his torso down, stacking Peter's legs over his head, and steps around to the left using his shoulders to push and clear the legs out of the way.

OPTIONAL TECHNIQUES

Passing the Guard -3, 38, 40, 41, 44, 45, 58, 71

FOLLOW UP TECHNIQUES

Side Mount-4, 5, 10, 11, 26, 28, 31, 46, 54, 65, 66, 86

PASSING THE GUARD WITH THE NEAR SIDE LEG THROUGH

Another way to pass the guard is presented here, the near side leg through. This pass has the advantage of blocking the triangle and other guard attacks as your knee, stuck between the opponent's legs, blocks his hips and creates distance between you and him, disabling most attack options. Greg uses the same method to break the guard as before (with the knee in the tailbone), so we pick up from there.

1 Greg breaks open Peter's legs with the knee in the tailbone method. Since he used his left knee on Peter's tailbone, Greg drops his right knee to the mat and raises his left one, placing the shin in front of Peter's hips. Greg starts to press forward, driving his left knee to the ground and pushing it over Peter's right thigh.

2 Greg slides his right hand and under-hooks Peter's left thigh as he drops his left knee to the mat, leaving his foot hooked over Peter's thigh, and reaches with his left arm to grab around Peter's head.

3 While still using his left arm around Peter's head to control the upper body and his right arm under Peter's left leg to control the lower body, Greg loops his right leg over his left, landing with the foot on the mat. Greg's hips now face towards Peter's feet. Having cleared his right leg from Peter's legs, Greg can let go of his left foot hook. He switches his hips by bringing the left leg under the right, reaching side control.

REVERSE **3** Notice how Greg drops his left knee to the ground but leaves his foot hooked over Peter's thigh to prevent Peter from locking his legs around Greg's right leg and trapping it in half-guard. Greg loops his right leg over the top of his left one, ending up with his hips facing towards Peter's feet.

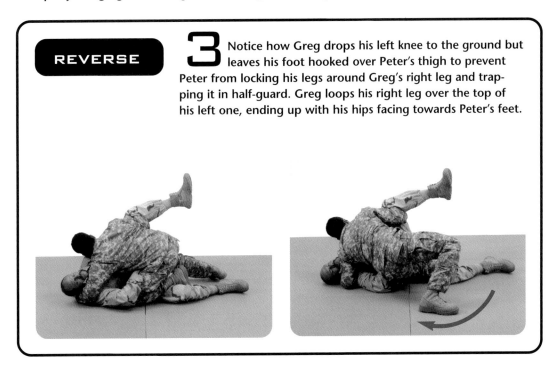

OPTIONAL TECHNIQUES

Passing the Guard -3, 38, 39, 41, 44, 45, 58, 71

FOLLOW UP TECHNIQUES

Side Mount-4, 5, 10, 11, 26, 28, 31, 46, 54, 65, 66, 86

PASSING THE GUARD WITH THE FAR SIDE LEG THROUGH

At times, when trying to use the near leg side through, your opponent may block your path on that side, making it difficult to proceed. In that case, don't fight with power. Instead, simply slide the knee to the opposite side for the far side leg through method. Some fighters prefer to use this variation directly, as they feel more comfortable with this pass. Additionally this may be the preferred way to pass if your opponent turns his body to the side away from the knee that is raised. In this case, since the left knee is up, Peter may turn his body to the right to block Greg's knee from going over his right leg.

1 Greg has his left knee up with the shin blocking Peter's hips. Greg's hands grip Peter's pants and his elbows are tight against his body and inside Peter's thighs. Peter uses his right hand on Greg's left shoulder to block Greg's advance on that side. Greg changes strategy and drives his left knee over Peter's left thigh. At the same time, he uses his left arm to under-hook Peter's right arm and pulls Peter's left arm with his right hand.

2 Greg continues to drive his left knee forward while pulling Peter's left arm up. Notice that Greg kept his foot hooked over Peter's left leg to prevent him from trapping the leg. Greg loops his right leg over Peter's leg, planting the foot wide and in line with his left knee. He pushes off it to drive his chest forward, pressing Peter's back to the ground. Notice how Greg pulling left Peter's arm up further forces Peter's back flat on the ground.

3 Greg steps forward with his right leg while still pressing Peter's back to the ground until he reaches 90° with Peter's body. He then releases his left foot from hooking the thigh and gets his hips facing down, ending up in side control.

OPTIONAL TECHNIQUES

Passing the Guard -3, 38, 39, 40, 44, 45, 58, 71

FOLLOW UP TECHNIQUES

Side Mount-4, 5, 10, 11, 26, 28, 31, 46, 54, 65, 66, 86

DEFENSE AGAINST PUNCHES IN THE GUARD 1

Having an opponent in your guard does not necessarily mean you are safe from his attacks. Many fighters use what is called "ground and pound", delivering punches from inside the guard to exert damage to their opponents. Being able to defend from these punches is a must. Here we present two different options to defend from punches in the guard. In the first one, you are able to maintain the closed guard by pulling the opponent forward with your legs.

1 Peter is inside Greg's guard and attempts to throw punches. In order to throw the punches, Peter has to extend his body and cock his arm back. Greg extends his body, driving Peter back with his hips to maintain distance between himself and Peter and take away some of the effectiveness of the blows. Greg positions his arms in front of his face to block the punches.

2 Peter persists in delivering the punches. Greg takes advantage of Peter's lunging forward for his punch and quickly coils his legs in, bringing his knees towards his head and forcing Peter to fall forward. Since Peter was throwing a right, he will generally end up with his right arm over Greg's head and his left arm blocked by Greg's right arm.

3 Greg quickly underhooks his left arm around Peter's right arm while using his right arm to grab Peter's head. He locks his hands together so his arms trap Peter's arm and head, keeping him close.

4 If Peter's right arm ends up below Greg's head, Greg overhooks Peter's right arm with his left arm and control the head with his right arm wrapped around it. Again, this keeps Peter close so he cannot rear back and start throwing punches again.

OPTIONAL TECHNIQUES

Guard-13, 14, 15, 32, 33, 34, 35, 36, 37, 43, 62, 63, 64, 65, 66, 67, 68, 69, 70

DEFENSE AGAINST PUNCHES IN THE GUARD 2

At times, the opponent doesn't fully commit himself and punches with more control and without leaning back so much. In that case, this option may be better.

1 Peter tries to punch Greg from inside the guard. Greg has his arms bent and in front of his face blocking the punches. With a right punch coming, Greg opens his legs and pushes off his feet, escaping his hips to the left. Greg raises his left arm and brings his left leg up so the elbow and the knee touch, creating a barrier with his leg and forearm.

2 Having blocked Peter's punch, Greg places his left foot on Peter's right hip and uses his knee in front of Peter's torso to control the distance. He then grabs Peter's right triceps with his left hand to prevent him from pulling it back and punching again, and re-centers his body.

a
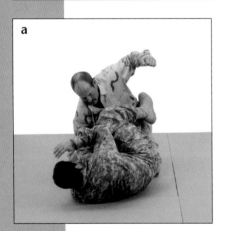

b
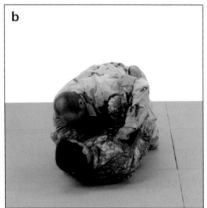

c
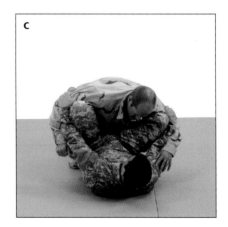

3 Peter coils his left arm and readies for a punch. Greg pushes off his feet, escapes his hips to the right and repeats the same motion to block and control Peter's left arm. Greg ends up with both feet on Peter's hips and the hands grabbing behind Peter's triceps to prevent him from punching.

4 Should Peter be very strong and stubborn, he may try to lean back and pry himself away from Greg's control. Greg then extends his legs and pushes Peter away with his feet. Notice that after Peter stands up, Greg keeps one foot touching Peter's hip to control the distance while the other leg is cocked and ready to deliver a front kick should Peter manage to get too close.

SIDE VIEW From here, Greg is ready to keep Peter away and stand up in base when the opportunity presents itself.

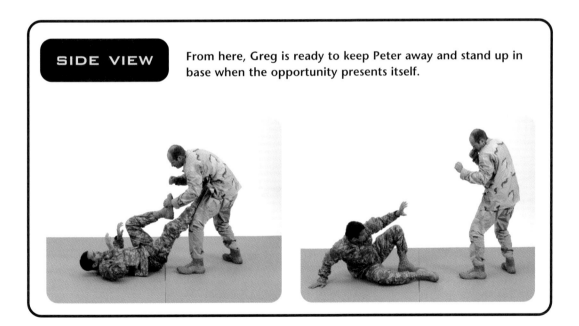

OPTIONAL TECHNIQUES

Guard-13, 14, 15, 32, 33, 34, 35, 36, 37, 42, 62, 63, 64, 65, 66, 67, 68, 69, 70

PASSING THE GUARD WITH PUNCHES: *Legs open*

One great way to open an opponent's guard in a street fight is to stand up and deliver punches. If he doesn't react and opens his guard, he will have to absorb tremendous punishment. An alert fighter will take advantage of his opponent's predicament and pass his guard in this fashion.

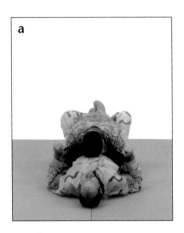
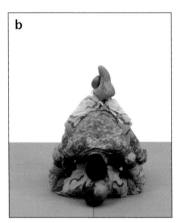

1 Greg is inside Peter's closed guard. His hands cup over Peter's biceps preventing him from punching Greg. Greg leans forward to put his weight on his chest and hands and pushes off them first to spring to his toes and then to stand up. Greg has each foot just wide of Peter's hips. His knees are pushing in so his legs trap Peter's legs and hips, taking away any movement. Greg's arms are also tight against his body with his elbows, pushing down on his own thighs. This adds even more pressure and control to trapping Peter's thighs. Greg turns his body slightly to his right by bringing the left knee forward. Greg has his left hand on Peter's mid-section to help his base and prevent him from falling forward.

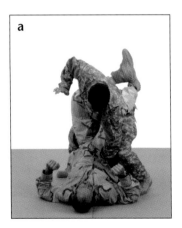
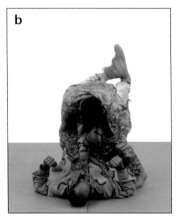

2 Greg coils his right arm and delivers an open palm strike to Peter's face (he may choose to punch instead), forcing Peter to unlock his legs, open his guard and bring his knees in front of Greg to defend against further punches. Greg raises his torso and pushes his hips forward with his knees and thighs still pressing in, forcing Peter's legs over his head.

3 Greg continues to lean forward and down, forcing Peter's legs back with his hips as he leans back and reaches with his right arm around Peter's left leg.

a

b

c

4 Greg drops his body down with his right knee, dropping towards the ground as he reaches with his right hand and grabs Peter's right collar. Greg pulls his left arm out from between Peter's legs and uses his left hand to grab the back of Peter's pants at the buttocks. Greg stacks Peter's legs over his head by dropping his weight forward and on top of the legs while pulling his torso down with his right arm. Greg extends his right leg back and continues to press down on Peter's legs as he walks around to his right, using his shoulders to push Peter's legs away and reach side control.

OPTIONAL TECHNIQUES

Passing the Guard -3, 38, 39, 40, 41, 45, 58, 71

FOLLOW UP TECHNIQUES

Side Mount-4, 5, 10, 11, 26, 28, 31, 46, 54, 65, 66, 86

PASSING THE GUARD WITH LEGS LOCKED

At times, your opponent will not open his legs even when being struck and will prefer to take the punishment rather than open his legs; or you may not want to punch your opponent to open his guard and pass. In that case, this is a great way to open the guard. The key to this pass is to stand in base and force your hips forward to maintain base and posture.

1 Greg springs to his feet as in the previous technique. His knees are pointing in so his thighs are pressing against Peter's legs. Greg drives his hips forward, turns his shoulders to the right, reaches back with his right arm and slides his hand under Peter's left leg.

OPTIONAL TECHNIQUES

Passing the Guard -3, 38, 39, 40, 41, 44, 58, 71

FOLLOW UP TECHNIQUES

Side Mount-4, 5, 10, 11, 26, 28, 31, 46, 54, 65, 66, 86

2 Greg slides his right arm between his and Peter's legs, resting his hand on the top of his thigh as he steps forward with his right foot slightly to re-center his body. At this point, although it may appear that Greg is vulnerable to the triangle, he actually isn't – he controls Peter's right leg and hip with his left arm and thigh pressing against it, taking away its mobility and any possibility of an attack. Greg takes a small step to his right with his right leg, forcing Peter to break his legs open. Greg raises his right elbow up, driving Peter's left leg up with it. Notice that Greg is still trapping Peter's right leg with his left leg and arm.

3 Greg grabs Peter's left thigh with his right arm. This controls the leg and foils the triangle attack. Greg drops his right knee down, brings his left elbow in front of Peter's hips and reaches with his right hand to grip Peter's right collar. Greg continues the pass as he did in the previous technique by stacking Peter's legs over his head and walking around to the right.

STRIKES FROM SIDE CONTROL

As we previously stated, side control is a great position to deliver strikes from because of the stability of the position. The introduction of strikes will open up opportunities to advance your position, such as mounting your opponent, as Greg demonstrates here.

1 Greg has side control on Peter. Since he is on Peter's left side, Greg's left arm wraps around Peter's head and his right arm underhooks Peter's left arm. The elbow is tight against Peter's left hip with the right knee under Peter's right thigh to take away his hip's mobility. Peter has good defensive posture with his right elbow on the ground and the forearm blocking Greg's hip.

a

2 Greg's first movement is to clear Peter's right forearm as he turns his hips counter-clockwise by sliding the left knee down towards Peter's feet until his thigh clears Peter's elbow. Once his thigh clears the elbow, Greg pushes his knee against Peter's side and slides the knee back towards his head, opening and clearing Peter's right arm out of the way.

b

c

OPTIONAL TECHNIQUES

4, 5, 10, 11, 26, 28, 31, 54, 65, 66, 86

FOLLOW UP TECHNIQUES

Mount-7, 10, 11, 12, 26, 27, 28, 54, 65, 66, 86

ANATOMY OF TECHNIQUES

J) Torso

3 Greg places his right palm on the ground and rears his right leg back and up and thrusts it down, striking Peter's right side with a knee strike.

a

b

4 Greg prepares another knee strike but this time Peter turns to his right and tries to block it by curling his left leg in. Greg takes advantage of this and slides his right knee over Peter's stomach and mounts him.

c

REVERSE **4** Notice how Greg slides his right knee over Peter's stomach and loops the foot over the legs to reach the mount.

DROP TO THE SINGLE LEG:
Superman double leg takedown

Being able to take the adversary to the ground is a necessity for one to be a complete fighter. While most direct takedowns work against inexperienced opponents, one cannot expect to only face inexperienced fighters in the battlefield or on the streets. Therefore it is important to be able to switch between takedown techniques in reaction to the opponent's counter to your initial attempt.

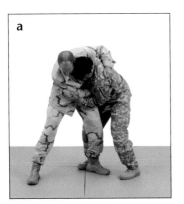
a

b

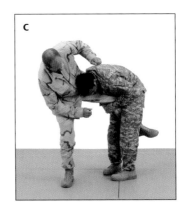
c

1 Greg has clinched Peter, his right arm encircling Peter's back with the hand gripping the right hip while his left hand grabs and pulls Peter's left elbow across his body, perhaps in preparation to execute a hip throw. Peter leans and tries to step away, making it difficult for Greg to step in front with his right leg and go for the hip throw. Greg quickly switches to the single leg by dropping his body down and wrapping Peter's left leg with both arms with the hands clasped together just above the knee. Greg pulls his arms tight against his chest, cinching the grip, and extends his legs, bringing Peter's left leg up. Greg closes his legs around Peter's leg and readies for the single leg takedown.

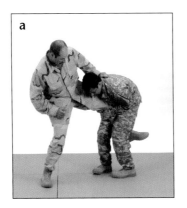
a

b

2 Peter counters Greg's single leg attempt (stepping back and pulling Peter's leg with him while driving the chest down on the thigh) by hopping towards Greg with the right leg. Seeing Peter's reaction, Greg changes to the double-leg as he times Peter's next hop. He lets go of his grip on the left leg and lunges down with both arms open and grabs Peter's right leg.

c

d

Greg pulls Peter's legs in, while at the same time he drives his shoulders against the left thigh, forcing Peter to fall.

DUMP

Once you have control over your opponent's legs there are many options to take him down, depending on his actions and reactions. One such takedown is the dump. It is best used when the opponent simply balances himself on one leg without much reaction to your single leg grab.

1 Greg has secured control of Peter's left leg with his arms around it, pulling the thigh tight against his chest and his legs clasped around the calf area.

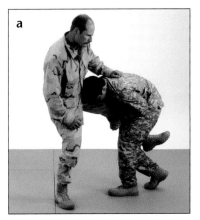

a

b

2 Greg takes a circular step to his left with his right foot, rotating his body in a clockwise direction. In the spinning motion, Greg's chest pushes Peter's thigh down and to the right while the back of his thigh presses against the right side of Peter's heel, forcing him to fall back and to the right.

c

TREETOP

Another alternative to the dump is the treetop. In the treetop, instead of using a circular motion to take your opponent down, you simply raise his leg up and throw it high, forcing him to fall. This may not be the best option against an opponent that is much taller than you and has good flexibility as you may not be able to lift his leg high enough to cause him to lose the balance. In that case, you should either use the dump, or add a right foot kick to the back of his right heel to help take away his base.

1 Greg has control over Peter's left leg as in the previous technique. When Peter hops forward, Greg pulls away and takes a circular step back to his right with his left leg and slides his left hand down, grabbing under Peter's calf.

2 Greg changes the left arm grip from in front of Peter's leg to under it by sliding his left arm between his chest and Peter's leg, holding it under the calf.

3 Greg steps to his right and heaves Peter's left leg up with his arms, causing him to fall.

BLOCK THE FAR KNEE

Another common reaction to the single leg counter is for your opponent to hook his foot on your leg to regain his balance and then try to pull away. In that case you can block his far knee and trip him forward.

1 Greg has secured Peter's left leg in a single leg grab. Peter hooks his foot on Greg's thigh to regain his balance and then tries to turn away and escape the grab.

2 Greg reaches with his right arm between Peter's legs and places the palm of his hand on Peter's right thigh just above the knee, blocking his ability to step forward. Greg then steps forward with his left leg and drives his chest against Peter's left thigh, pushing it down while lifting the lower part of the leg and forcing him to fall forward.

3 Greg continues to block the knee with his right hand and follows Peter's fall, stepping outside of his legs and ending up mounted on him.

HIP THROW

The hip throw is a very effective and devastating throw when properly executed. It is best applied in the clinch if you can keep the opponent close to you or if he stops after a scramble. The hip throw is most effective if the opponent's body is bent forward instead of standing straight up. You can use a knee to the stomach to induce him to bend down. It is very important for the hip throw to properly step in front of the opponent's hips with your hip and to keep your legs bent and square in front of him. This will give you better control over his body and prevent a possible injury from him falling down on your outside leg.

1 Greg clinches Peter. His right arm is wrapped around Peter's back with the hand gripping Peter's right hip and his left arm trapping Peter's right arm. Greg's legs are bent with his hips perpendicular to Peter's hips. His feet are open shoulder width for base.

2 Greg points his left foot forward and steps back with his right leg to create space between his hips and Peter's. He then steps with the right leg in front of Peter, making sure that his feet are parallel and inside of Peter's feet. Greg pays particular attention to locking his hips in front of Peter's hips by edging them slightly outside of Peter's hips. This will allow Greg more control over Peter's body as he executes the throw. Greg bends his knees slightly more and bends his body down at the waist.

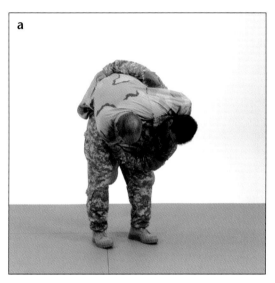

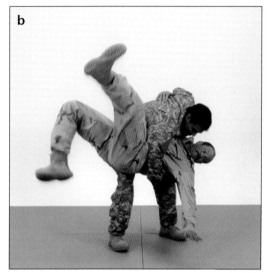

3 Greg executes the hip throw by extending his legs, thus thrusting Peter's body up. At the same time, he pulls Peter's right arm across with his left hand and rotates his shoulders to the left, twisting Peter's body as it falls over to the ground. Notice how important Greg's leg position is: as Peter falls down, if his right leg (outside) is not lined up inside Peter's right leg and his hips slightly out, Peter may fall on Greg's right leg, buckling the knee.

DEFENSE AGAINST THE STANDING GUILLOTINE: *Jumping around the side*

As we stated earlier, the standing guillotine is a devastating choke when properly applied. While you may be aware of the attack and try to avoid it in a clinch, at times you may make a mistake and get caught by it. Therefore it is very important to know how to defend it.

1 Greg is caught in a standing guillotine by Peter. Greg's immediate concern is to defend his neck from being choked. He reaches with his right hand in a claw grip (all five fingers together) and hooks and pulls down on Peter's left wrist, while at the same time he loops his left arm over Peter's right shoulder, making sure the crease of his arm hooks over the top of the shoulder. Greg now has defended his neck – Peter cannot apply any additional pressure by arching his body back as he will simply bring Greg with him.

DETAIL

1 Greg reaches and inserts his right hand over the top of Peter's left wrist. Greg may be able to actually break Peter's grip by twisting Peter's wrist as he pulls it down.

2 Having defended his neck, Greg places his right hand on Peter's left knee and pushes off it to jump to his left. Greg ends up with his hips perpendicular to Peter's hips and his left leg behind Peter's right leg. Greg delivers a short knee strike with his left knee hitting the back of Peter's right knee, causing the leg to buckle and Peter to fall back. Greg steps out with his left leg and controls Peter's fall (since Peter still controls his head, he doesn't want Peter to just slam to the ground).

3 Greg falls across Peter with his left hand planted next to the right side of Peter's head and the right hand planted next to his left hip. Greg wants to make sure Peter doesn't turn to his left and roll Greg over with him. Having established his base, Greg reaches with his left hand and grabs Peter's left shoulder, making sure the forearm is in front of Peter's neck. Greg extends his left leg back and turns his hips in a clockwise direction. He drops his weight on his left elbow, pressing his forearm on Peter's throat and forcing him to let go of his grip around Greg's head.

DEFENSE AGAINST STANDING GUILLOTINE: *Defending knee strikes*

Be aware of the possibility of knee strikes from the enemy when you are caught in a standing guillotine, especially if he bends you down. Or, if you kick the opponent to try to make him let go of the choke as a desperate way to defend the guillotine, you actually cause him to strike back. In that case use this technique.

1 Peter has Greg in a standing guillotine and presses his head down. This is the prelude to delivering knee strikes to Greg's face.

2 Greg places his hands in front of Peter's thigh, blocking the knee strikes. Notice that Greg's hands form a "U" with the ends of the palms touching each other and the fingers open so as to cup the thigh. Greg steps forward with his left leg, making sure his foot lands in line with and between Greg's feet.

3 Greg steps forward with his right leg, his foot lands past Peter's feet as he sits down. Greg's hands are still blocking Peter's left knee and preventing him from stepping forward. Peter needs to let go of his guillotine or he will be thrown forward.

REVERSE

3 Peter doesn't let go of his guillotine grip and gets his face smashed on the ground. Attention: When practicing, make sure your partner lets go of the grip and braces his fall to avoid hitting his face on the ground.

KNEE ON THE STOMACH

The knee on the stomach is a very strong and dynamic position for a combat situation. With your knee pressing down on the enemy's gut, you can quickly drain his energy (the pressure of the knee on the stomach alone drains energy) while at the same time you can deliver punches, and introduce or control a weapon situation. Achieving the knee on the stomach is shown here. The key to reaching the knee on the stomach is to maintain pressure on your arms, pinning the enemy down as you prop your body up.

1 Greg has side control on Peter. His left hand reaches over Peter's head to grab the collar next to the ear. His right hand presses down on Peter's left hip. In one movement, Greg pushes off his arms, raising his body, and slides the right knee on top of Peter's stomach. He plants the left foot wide so his knee is pointing up and the leg is semi-extended.

ALTERNATIVE

2 Alternatively, Greg may use this grip. His right hand grabs Peter's right pants leg and his left hand grabs the right side of the collar. Greg jumps to the knee on the stomach, his right hand pulling on Peter's right pant leg to add pressure on his knee and keeping Peter pinned to the ground. From this grip Greg cannot deliver punches. However he exerts great pressure on Peter's stomach, undermining his resistance.

REVERSE

2 Notice Greg's preparation to reach the knee on the stomach variation: his right knee is tight against Peter's left hip and his right hand grabs the right pant leg. As he springs to the position, his right knee easily slides over Peter's stomach while the right hand pulls Peter's right leg up, forcing Greg's own body down and adding a lot of pressure to the right knee on Peter's stomach.

a

b

c

PAPER CUTTER CHOKE FROM THE KNEE IN THE STOMACH

A great choke from the knee on the stomach is the paper cutter choke. The paper cutter is a choke that is very quick to achieve. Here, Greg takes advantage of the controlling grip on Peter's collar with one hand by simply using his other hand to grab and pull Peter's lapel for the choke.

1 Greg has his right knee on Peter's stomach with his left hand grabbing Peter's left collar and the right hand pressing on the right hip. Greg uses his right hand to open and straighten Peter's collar as he slides his left hand down the collar to tighten the grip. Notice Greg's forearm presses down against Peter's throat.

2 Greg's right hand grabs and pulls Peter's right collar to take the slack while he drives his left elbow to the ground, tightening the collar choke and also forcing his forearm against Peter's throat for a nasty choke.

DETAIL

2 Notice Greg's left hand grip on Peter's collar: the thumb is inside with the four fingers gripping the outside so the blade of his forearm presses against the throat. Also notice how Greg's right hand reaches inside Peter's right collar: this time, all four fingers are inside and the thumb out for a great grip pulling up. Greg drops his left elbow to the ground as he pulls the right collar with the right hand, tightening the collar around Peter's throat.

REVERSE BENT ARM-BAR FROM KNEE ON THE STOMACH

Many times, when faced with the knee on the stomach, the adversary in his struggle to escape the position will use his outside hand to push the knee away and try to relieve the pressure. This exposes that arm for the reverse bent arm-bar.

1 Greg has knee on the stomach with his right knee on Peter's gut. Peter uses his left hand to try to push Greg's knee away and escape the position. Greg immediately grabs and controls Peter's left wrist with his right hand and uses the weight of his body to push it down, pinning it to the ground.

a

b

2 Greg gets off the knee on the stomach position and back to side control as he drops his knees to the ground. He reaches with his left hand under Peter's arm around the triceps area and grabs his own right wrist with his left hand, locking the figure 4 grip on Peter's arm. Greg steps out and over Peter's head with his left foot so his thigh will block the head as he applies the reverse bent arm-bar torque. He applies the bent arm-bar by pushing Peter's wrist back with his right arm while using the left arm to pull the left shoulder up, torquing the arm around the shoulder socket.

c

STRAIGHT ARM-BAR FROM KNEE ON THE STOMACH

Often times, because they aren't used to the suffocating pressure, the victim of the knee on the stomach gets so desperate to escape the torture that he will extend his arm and try to push the attacker away. Be ready for this common reaction and apply the straight arm-bar.

1 Greg has knee on stomach with his right knee pressing on Peter's gut and his left arm pulling up on Peter's right arm for control. Peter tries to use his right hand to push away Greg's shoulder in an attempt to release the knee pressure and escape the position.

2 Greg pulls up on Peter's right arm, turning him towards his left, and leans forward over Peter's torso with his body. Greg steps over Peter's head with his left leg making sure his foot lands very close to the left side of Peter's face, taking away any space for him to move his head and escape. Greg continues to pull Peter's right arm up with his left hand and drops his hips down so his pelvis presses against the back of Peter's elbow.

3 Greg drops down to the mat as he grabs Peter's right wrist with both hands. He then extends his body, dropping his back to the mat and extending Peter's right arm. Greg raises his hips pressing his pelvis against Peter's left elbow, hyper-extending the joint.

ALTERNATIVE **3** Greg uses his right hand to grab and pull on Peter's right pant leg as he drops to the ground to execute the arm-bar. By pulling Peter's right leg up, Greg takes away Peter's ability to push off the right leg and arch his body to try to escape the submission.

STRAIGHT ANKLE LOCK

At times when trying to pass your adversary's guard – whether in combat situation or in a street fight – you can quickly end the situation with the straight ankle lock. The straight ankle lock can be a vicious submission that can render your opponent incapacitated and inflict a great deal of pain by attacking the ankle joint. Be careful when drilling this with a partner as the joint may be damaged before he feels significant amounts of pain.

1 Greg is attempting to pass Peter's guard. Peter has his left leg up. Greg has his left hand on Peter's stomach for base; his left leg is between Peter's legs with the shinbone pressing against the pelvic bone to maintain distance. Greg's right leg is outside of Peter's left leg. Greg wraps his right arm around Peter's left calf.

2 Greg twists his right leg so that his right foot pushes against Peter's left hip with the heel facing up and the toes pointing out. Since he is attacking Peter's left leg, Greg drops down to the mat on his right side. Greg pinches his legs together to trap Peter's leg in. Notice that Greg's left shinbone will stop Peter's attempt to defend the submission by trying to sit up and get over the top of Greg.

3 Greg brings his left arm back, grabs his left wrist with his right hand and places his left hand on top of Peter's shin, completing the figure 4 lock around the ankle. Greg then arches his torso back to apply the pressure on the ankle with the back of his right armpit, pushing Peter's toes back and pivoting the foot around the ankle joint for the submission. It is very important that Greg adjusts his figure 4 lock before he goes for the submission. Greg wants to have his armpit as close to the top of Peter's foot as possible and his right forearm under Peter's Achilles tendon for best leverage.

GROUND TECHNIQUES

While MAC I and MAC II give you the basic and intermediate techniques and the fundamentals of fighting in the battle-field or as a police officer in a violent street confrontation, H2H Ground Techniques explore more advanced techniques for combat fighting. These are the same techniques that Greg Thompson teaches the US Special Forces. Over his career as an instructor, Thompson, with feedback from real soldiers coming back from real live battlefield combat situations, has modified and perfected his H2H program into the ultimate combative fighting system.

MOUNTED KNEE ELBOW

Having multiple options to escape a difficult position like the mount is always a good thing. The knee to elbow is a solid escape that is best used when the opponent is not delivering punches but rather trying to stabilize or pause before attacking.

Note: This technique will help you learn to use your feet in a scramble, freeing up your hands.

1 Peter is mounted on Greg. Greg has his elbows close to his body. He chooses to escape to his left, so he drops his left leg flat on the ground and curls the right leg with the foot firmly planted on the ground. Greg's right forearm is in front of Peter's hips while the left elbow is firmly set on the ground so the forearm is in front of Peter's right thigh. Greg has his hands placed against Peter's right hip. Greg pushes off his right foot and turns to his left as he brings his left leg up towards his head, the knee sliding under Peter's right leg.

2 Greg hooks his right foot over Peter's right calf and pulls it to his right, trapping it. At this point, Peter's right leg is immobilized; his thigh is blocked by Greg's left forearm and the ankle is trapped by Greg's right leg.

3 Greg extends his arms to push Peter's hips slightly back as he coils his left leg in, sliding the thigh under Peter's knee. Greg ends up with his leg in front of Peter's right leg.

OPTIONAL TECHNIQUES

2, 6

FOLLOW UP TECHNIQUES

Mount-7, 10, 11, 12, 26, 27, 28, 54, 65, 66, 86

4 Greg pushes off his left foot and escapes his hips wide to the left as he slides his left arm under Peter's right armpit.

REVERSE

5 Reversing the angle for better view: Greg uses his right hand on Peter's left knee to block it as he coils his right leg in under Peter's hips until the knee comes out in front of the hips and the right foot hooks under Peter's left thigh. Greg slides his right arm under Peter's left armpit and pushes off his left foot to slide his hips to the right until his right foot escapes and he is able to lock his legs around Peter for full guard.

a

b

c

d

e

SIDE KNEE ELBOW

Being trapped in side control is not a good position to be in. Being able to quickly and effectively escape and replace the guard is very important in order to survive in a fight because of the leverage you gain to be able to transition to a weapon or retain your weapon. Escaping from side control is demonstrated here. Greg uses the same principles as in the previous escape; escaping the hip, coiling his leg and bringing the knee to the elbow to block his side and then replace the guard.

a

b

c

1 Peter has side control on Greg. Greg has his left forearm in front of Peter's right hip to maintain distance and the right arm is under Peter's left armpit. Pushing off his right foot, Greg escapes his hips to the right and coils his left leg in so his knee slides in front of Peter's hips, coming out the outside of the right hip. The foot locks outside Peter's left hip.

REVERSE

1 Check out Greg's left arm position: the elbow is on the ground and the forearm is in front of Peter's hip to maintain distance.

OPTIONAL TECHNIQUES

20, 21, 61

FOLLOW UP TECHNIQUES

Guard-13, 14, 15, 32, 33, 34, 35, 36, 37, 42, 43, 62, 63, 64, 65, 66, 67, 68, 69, 70

2 Greg continues to push off his right foot and slides his hips to the left as he drops the left foot down. As Greg slides to his left, his left knee blocks Peter from regaining side control. Greg turns his body to his right as his hips reach outside Peter's body and hooks his right leg on Peter's left side.

3 With his hips way wide and his body turned to the right, Greg is able to unhook his left foot from Peter's right thigh and loop it around the back, locking his feet on Peter's back. He has successfully replaced the guard.

ALTERNATIVE

a

Alternatively, Greg may choose to hook his right foot inside of Peter's left thigh for extra control. He will then extend that leg, pushing Peter's legs away to create space to slide his left foot under the hips and replace the open guard

b

c

SIDE MOUNT ARM-BAR

A great attack from the bottom when someone has side mount on you is the arm-bar. Greg demonstrates the attack here and continues on in the event that the adversary escapes his arm-bar.

1 Peter is on Greg's right side on side mount. Greg puts his right hand on Peter's left hip and with the straight arm keeps distance. Greg escapes his hips to the left and grabs Peter's right elbow with his left hand.

a

b

c

2 While still controlling Peter's right arm, Greg slides his right knee in front of Peter's chest, making sure the shin blocks the chest. He raises his hips and loops the left leg over Peter's head. Greg grabs Peter's right wrist with both hands and extends his body, driving his hips up against Peter's elbow and hyper-extending it for the arm-bar.

REVERSE

2 Notice how Greg's left foot hooks on Peter's right side, preventing him from moving away, while the left leg weighs down on the head. This forces Peter to lean to his right as Greg extends his legs for the arm-bar.

3 Peter may be able to yank his arm out by moving his elbow past Greg's hips and negating the arm-bar. Should Peter be able to bring his right arm completely out, he may be in position to deliver punches to Greg's face. So Greg coils his left leg, placing the foot in front of Peter's throat. This will keep proper distance and defend against the punches.

a

b

4 Greg pushes Peter's face away with the left leg. As he gets enough space, he places the right foot on Peter's left hip to help push him away. Greg extends his legs in an explosive motion sending Peter falling away.

c

OPTIONAL TECHNIQUES

20, 21, 60

ANATOMY OF TECHNIQUES

H) Elbow Separation

ARM CHOKE CLIMB AROUND

When controlling your enemy in the guard, at times you may be able to control his wrists and prevent him from grabbing onto anything. This kind of control gives you many attacking options, like the triangle, a key-lock or the arm choke climb around as demonstrated here. The key to this move is to keep his hands away and prevent him from being able to regain a grip so you can move around him. Note: Thompson's rule for weapon transition, retention and takeaways: *Always go to the weapon side.*

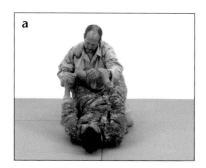  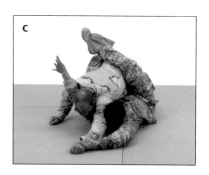

1 Greg has Peter in his closed guard. Greg controls Peter's wrists with his hands and prevents him from regaining a grip by pushing the arms back. Peter leans forward to counter Greg's push. Greg, in one swift move, brings his legs towards his head while he pulls Peter's wrists up over his head and towards his left, forcing Peter to fall forward. Greg makes sure that Peter's left elbow is past his left ear before he releases his left hand grip on Peter's right wrist to wrap the arm around Peter's head while pressing his head against Peter's left triceps. It is imperative for Greg to push his head against Peter's triceps to prevent him from bringing the left arm around in front of Greg's face and blocking the move to the back.

2 Greg locks his hands together, pulling the arms together and squeezing Peter's head and left arm between his left arm and head. He then opens his legs, plants the right foot on the ground and pushes off it to slide his hips to the right until his body is almost perpendicular to Peter's body.

3 Greg may decide to go for the choke. He grabs the inside of his right arm at the biceps with the left hand and bends the right arm so his hand reaches Peter's forehead. Greg re-locks his feet and applies the choking pressure for the arm and head triangle by pulling his arms in and bringing his elbows together while pushing his head towards Peter's head. Greg's head pushes Peter's left arm against the left side of his neck while Greg's left arm presses the right side of Peter's neck for the choke.

ALTERNATIVE

a

b

c

3 In the event there are weapons involved: in this case, Peter has a pistol on his left side. Greg should always drive Peter's body away from his gun side, in this case the left side, so he can block and control Peter's left arm from reaching the gun. At this point, Greg can easily take and use Peter's pistol against him.

4 Alternatively, Greg may prefer to continue to Peter's back instead of attempting the choke. He may do so because he cannot get a good grip for the head and arm triangle or simply because he wants to get a better controlling position before deciding which way to finish his adversary. He will not do this if Peter has a weapon! Instead, he would use the previous option. Greg reaches with his right hand and grabs Peter's right wing (just inside the armpit). Greg pulls himself up on Peter's back with his right hand and slides his body around Peter's until he is on his back. Greg makes sure he stays tight against Peter during the whole process and keeps his head pushed against Peter's left arm until he is clear on Peter's back.

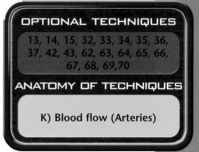

OPTIONAL TECHNIQUES
13, 14, 15, 32, 33, 34, 35, 36, 37, 42, 43, 62, 63, 64, 65, 66, 67, 68, 69,70

ANATOMY OF TECHNIQUES

K) Blood flow (Arteries)

REVERSE

4 Check out Greg's movement: he opens his legs as he grabs the inside of Peter's right armpit with his right hand. He then pulls himself around Peter while sliding the left leg on the ground. Greg loops the right leg over and hooks both heels in front of Peter's hips for back control.

5 Greg reaches with his right hand inside Peter's right arm and grabs the wrist to control the arm. He opens his left arm out, plants the hand wide of his shoulder, and pushes off it while pulling Peter's right wrist in to complete taking the back. Greg stretches his body and drives his hips down, forcing Peter to spread forward.

H2H
GROUND TECHNIQUES
TECHNIQUE 063

STAND UP DUMP BACK

At times you may get your opponent in an arm lock from the guard but he is able to stand up and get his elbow out defending the lock. Or you may not feel that the arm-lock is solid and you will lose your opponent. The dump back is a perfect option in these situations.

1 Greg attempts an arm-lock on Peter but Peter stands up. Notice that Greg's left calf is not pressing down on Peter's neck, giving Peter room to yank his arm out. Greg senses he is going to lose the submission and quickly changes to the dump back. Greg's right hand grabs the back of Peter's left ankle as he loops the left leg over Peter's head towards the right hip.

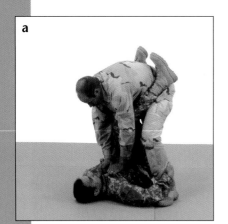 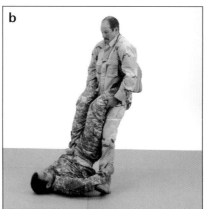 

2 As Greg completes the loop, his hips are on the ground, his hands hold the back of Peter's ankles and his heels press against Peter's thighs. Greg presses his heels down towards the ground. His calves push against Peter's thighs, forcing Peter to fall back. Notice that since Greg's hands hold the back of the heels, Peter cannot step back and regain his balance, so he is forced to fall.

3 It is important for Greg to move to one side in order to stay close to Peter as he goes to mount. If he tries to mount directly, he will have to go on his knees, allowing too much space for Peter to insert a knee or escape the hip. As Peter's back hits the ground, Greg plants the right hand back and turns his body to the right so his right foot and knee touch the mat. Greg continues to move forward and to his right. His right knee touches the ground, the hips sliding forward over Peter's stomach. He pulls Peter's left sleeve with his left hand so as to help himself move up and to prevent Peter from propping himself up on that arm. Greg continues to move towards Peter's head, helping himself by pushing with his right hand and pulling with the left until he is mounted on Peter.

FOLLOW UP TECHNIQUES

Mount-7, 10, 11, 12, 26, 27, 28, 54, 65, 66, 86

ELEVATOR

Many times, when the opponent is in your guard and ready to deliver a punch, you can quickly pull him forward with your legs (while, of course, protecting your face), break his posture and hook him up for the elevator sweep.

1 Peter is inside Greg's guard. He leans back and cocks his right hand to strike Greg's face. Greg raises his left arm, bent at the elbow with the forearm in front of his face, to block the punch.

2 Greg quickly pulls his legs up towards his head and curls his body in as if doing a sit up, bringing Peter forward. Greg wraps his arms under Peter's arms, locking the hands behind his back.

a

3 Greg escapes his hips to the left as he extends his left leg and raises the right leg up so his body turns to the right slightly, allowing him to loop and hook his left foot in front of Peter's right thigh.

b

c

4 Greg pushes off his feet and slides his hips back. He sits up and drops his right foot down, hooking it over Peter's left calf and trapping it. Greg's head needs to be under Peter's head with the face pressing against the chest. Greg wraps his right arm around Peter's left arm, with the hand touching his head, to prevent Peter from being able to open the arm out and block the reversal. Greg dips his right shoulder to the ground as he kicks the left leg up, elevating Peter's right leg and forcing him to roll over.

5 Greg ends up mounted on Peter and can immediately go for a bent arm-bar, if he chooses to, by locking the left hand on Peter's left wrist and grabbing his own left wrist with the right hand for the figure 4 lock on Peter's left arm. Greg applies the pressure by sliding Peter's wrist down the mat while raising the elbow, torquing the arm around the shoulder for the submission.

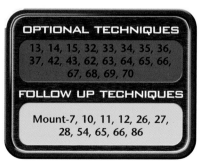

OPTIONAL TECHNIQUES

13, 14, 15, 32, 33, 34, 35, 36, 37, 42, 43, 62, 63, 64, 65, 66, 67, 68, 69, 70

FOLLOW UP TECHNIQUES

Mount-7, 10, 11, 12, 26, 27, 28, 54, 65, 66, 86

CLOTH CHOKES: *T-shirt on or off*

Being able to finish an opponent during a fight is a great asset to have, and what better way to finish a fight than by choking your opponent. Greg demonstrates a variety of ways to choke your opponent, whether he has a t-shirt or not.

A: From the guard

1 Greg has Peter in his closed guard. He keeps Peter close to his chest by holding the back of the head with his left arm. Greg grabs Peter's t-shirt with the right hand, pulling it up towards the head and bunching the shirt material near the top.

a

b

c

2 Greg reaches over Peter's head with his left hand and grabs the t-shirt. His thumb grabs inside the collar and the fingers grab around the tail of the t-shirt. Greg slips his right arm in front of Peter's chest so he can reach and grab the left side of the t-shirt with the right hand, but this time the fingers reach inside the collar and the thumb grabs the back of the shirt. Greg pumps his legs quickly, driving Peter back and forth so he can loop his left elbow around Peter's head so both forearms are in front in a choking position. Greg chokes Peter using the normal collar choke motion: bringing his elbows down along the side of his body and expanding his chest.

REVERSE

2 Notice how Greg wraps his hands around the entire t-shirt instead of just gripping a small part of it. This gives him a much better choking pressure. Also notice Greg's grips: for the left hand, the thumb goes inside the collar and the finger around the back of the t-shirt while the right is the opposite, the fingers grab inside the collar and the thumb grabs over the t-shirt.

B: From side control or half-guard

1 Greg has side control on Peter. He grabs and bunches up Peter's t-shirt with both hands.

2 Greg steps around to his left side towards Peter's head as he slides the right elbow across Peter's chest until the forearm pushes against the throat. Greg brings his elbows together. Greg continues stepping to his left until he reaches the north-south position with his body at 180° in relation to Peter's. Greg applies the choking pressure in a similar manner to the collar choke with the forearms pushing against Peter's throat. He drops his head to the ground next to Peter's right side and drives the right elbow towards the ground. The forearm pushes against the throat and the top of the left forearm pushes against the right side of Peter's throat.

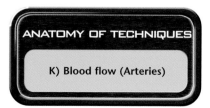

ANATOMY OF TECHNIQUES

K) Blood flow (Arteries)

C: From any position

Any kind of cloth you may have will do: a small towel, a belt,
part of a shirt or jacket, bed sheet or a rope.

1 Greg holds the towel with both hands. Greg doesn't want to hold too close to the end of the towel as his grip may slip. He also wants to have the hands somewhat close together – no more than four inches apart for the tightest choke. Greg's hands grip the towel with the top of the hand pointing to the same direction (both thumbs are up). Since Greg has his left hand grabbing the bottom of the towel, his left arm is below and in front of Peter's head.

2 Greg presses the right forearm on Peter's chest just under his chin with the hand touching Peter's right shoulder. Greg loops the left elbow around Peter's head.

3 He slides the forearm down close to the left side of the head and completes the choke loop, bringing the left elbow over the right arm. Greg chokes Peter using the same motion as the collar choke.

SLEEVE CHOKE

Sleeve chokes are very sneaky and effective. Because of the deceptiveness of the sleeve choke they are the prefect attack move in many situations. By using the sleeve cuff or a DEFENSEBAND™ (a self defense watch band, see page 255) as a pivot point, you can surprise and choke your opponent before he is even aware of how you are choking him. Look for the sleeve choke from many positions like side control, half-guard, guard and mount.

1 From a side clinch, Greg wraps his left arm around Peter's head, his hand touching the left shoulder. Greg reaches with his right arm towards Peter's left shoulder and grabs the inside cuff of his own sleeve with his left hand.

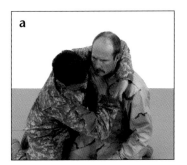
a

b

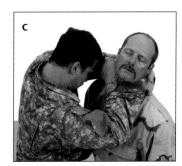
c

2 Greg pivots his right hand around the cuff so the lower blade of his hand touches the right side of Peter's neck. Greg makes a fist with his right hand to prevent Peter from grabbing and twisting his fingers as a defense to the choke. Greg then applies the choke by extending both arms. His left hand pulls the cuff forward, pressing against the left side of Peter's neck, while the right hand aims in the direction of Peter's right ear, pressing against the right side of the neck for the choke. This is a very powerful choke when properly applied and the opponent will either submit or quickly pass out.

3 From side control, Greg uses the same sleeve choke by wrapping the left arm under Peter's head. The hand holds inside the right cuff with the right fist on Peter's throat. Greg extends the arm for the choke.

4 From the closed guard.

5 From the half-guard bottom.

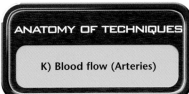
ANATOMY OF TECHNIQUES

K) Blood flow (Arteries)

GET TO YOUR FEET - HEAD UP

At times, you may just want to get to your feet after being on the ground, even with your opponent in your guard. Perhaps he is successfully striking you, or you feel you are superior on your feet, or you want to draw your pistol to control him. This is a great way to do that when the opponent has his head up and his back straight in posture. Always have your head on the weapon side.

1 Greg has Peter inside his guard. He unlocks his feet as he sits up, turning his body to his right and rolling forward, first on his elbow, then propping his right arm back. At the same time, Greg reaches with his left hand and grabs Peter's left shoulder with the forearm bent at the elbow and pressing against Peter's throat.

2 Greg blades his body to keep his weapon side away from Peter. His left forearm and hand keeps Peter from coming forward and helps protect Greg's weapon side. Greg plants his left foot on the ground and pushes off it while bracing off his right arm to raise his hips up and coil the right leg back under his own hips. Greg plants the right foot back past his right hand. He now has a 3-point stance with his feet and right hand providing base. Notice that throughout the entire movement, to stand up Greg keeps his right hand back for base and his left forearm pressing against Peter's throat. Greg also keeps his eyes on Peter, ready to react to any attacks he may try.

3 Greg turns his hips forward and grabs Peter's head with both hands. From here Greg can deliver a knee strike or use a choke to subdue Peter.

OPTIONAL TECHNIQUES
13, 14, 15, 32, 33, 34, 35, 36, 37, 42, 43, 62, 63, 64, 65, 66, 68, 69, 70

GET TO YOUR FEET - HEAD DOWN

In case your opponent has his head down for a low defensive posture, use this method to get to your feet.

1 Greg has Peter in his closed guard. This time however Peter has his head down close to Greg's chest in a low defensive posture. Peter has his elbows tight against his own thighs, taking away some of Greg's hip and leg movement. Since Peter's head is to Greg's right, Greg turns to his right and uses his hands to push Peter's head further to the right. Peter's neck cannot resist the push of both of Greg's arms, forcing him to lean in that direction and break his defensive posture.

2 Greg continues to push Peter's head with his hands as he opens his legs, slides his hips back and to the left, and slips his left knee in front of Peter's chest. Greg pushes Peter face down to the ground as he moves his torso and hips further away from Peter and to the left.

3 Greg plants the left foot on the ground and opens his right arm back, placing the right hand past his head for base. Greg continues to push Peter face down on the ground using his left hand only now. Using the same movement as standing in base (technique #1), Greg gets to his feet by pushing off his left foot, bringing the right leg under the hips and planting the right foot past his right hand for his 3-point base.

OPTIONAL TECHNIQUES

3, 14, 15, 32, 33, 34, 35, 36,
37, 42, 43, 62, 63, 64, 65, 66,
67, 69, 70

GET TO YOUR FEET TRANSITION TO KNEE STRIKE AND CHOKE

Once Greg gets to his feet, many attack options may appear, such as a knee strike if the opponent stays back, or a guillotine choke if he reaches forward and grabs Greg's leg in an attempt to keep him close.

1 Greg stands up and Peter stays back. Greg turns his hips forward, grabs Peter's head with both hands and pulls it down as he launches his right knee forward, striking Peter's chin.

a

b

REVERSE

2 Should Peter try to reach and grab Greg's left (forward) leg with both arms, Greg reaches with his left arm (same side as the leg) and wraps it around Peter's neck so his hand comes out the right side. Greg then grabs his own left wrist with his right hand and tightens the noose around Peter's neck, setting up the guillotine choke lock. Greg sits back and wraps his legs around Peter's body, closing the guard. When his back touches the ground, Greg extends his legs, pushing Peter's body away while he pulls his left forearm up against Peter's throat for the choke.

c

OPTIONAL TECHNIQUES
13, 14, 15, 32, 33, 34, 35, 36,
37, 42, 43, 62, 63, 64, 65, 66,
67, 68, 70

GET TO YOUR FEET TRANSITION TO SHOULDER LOCK

At times, your opponent (perhaps in an attempt to go for your weapon) may try to grab both your legs and he may keep his head very tight against your body, making it difficult to reach around with your arm for the guillotine choke. In that case, a great option is the shoulder lock.

1 Peter tries to grab both of Greg's legs while keeping his head tight and to the outside of Greg's body. This makes it very hard for Greg to execute the guillotine. Greg leans forward, pushing his left knee against Peter's chest to hold him back and remain in base. Although he can apply the shoulder lock to either arm, he will do it on the arm that is extended the most since he will have more leverage. He grabs Peter's left wrist with his right hand. He turns his torso further to the right so he can overhook his left arm around Peter's left arm and grab his own right wrist with his left hand, locking the figure-4 on Peter's left arm. Greg makes sure to keep this lock tight against his right leg as he will use the power of his turning body to force Peter's arm around.

OPTIONAL TECHNIQUES

13, 14, 15, 32, 33, 34, 35, 36, 37, 42, 43, 62, 63, 64, 65, 66, 67, 68, 69

a

b

c

2 Greg pivots off his left foot and steps forward with the right leg so his right foot is just past Peter's knee. He then sits down on the mat with his legs pressing against Peter's legs. He escapes his hips and turns his body to his left, driving Peter's left arm back and around with his arms. Greg continues to escape the hips and turn to his left as he locks his feet behind Peter's back. Greg continues to torque Peter's arm around the shoulder for the submission.

GUARD ESCAPE

As the old saying goes: "There are many ways to skin a cat!" There are also many ways to pass the guard. In case of the open guard, one of the most effective ways is presented here. In this case, Greg controls Peter's feet and feints to one side and passes to the other. It is very important for Greg to control Peter's feet from this position. This allows him to push the legs to the side and pass, but more importantly, it prevents Peter from throwing a devastating heel strike to Greg's face.

1 Greg stands in front of Peter. His left leg is forward with the shin pressing on the back of Peter's right thigh and his left elbow presses down on his own left thigh forming a barrier, which prevents Peter from attacking him with a triangle, an arm-lock or even trying to close the half-guard. Greg's right hand pushes down on Peter's left knee as he tries to pass Peter's open guard. Greg needs to worry about Peter's heel kick.

2 Greg gains posture by standing erect while driving the left shin further forward, pressing it against the back of Peter's right thigh. Greg's hands grab the top of Peter's ankles. Greg takes a step back with his left leg and pulls Peter's ankles back, straightening the legs.

3 Greg feints a pass to Peter's left as he swings Peter's legs to the left. Peter expects Greg to pass to his left so he starts to turn in that direction. Greg then quickly throws Peter's legs to the right and steps forward with the left foot, reaching Peter's side. Greg steps forward with the right leg and places that knee on Peter's stomach, completing the guard pass. Greg is now in a great controlling position ready to strike, use a weapon or take control over Peter's weapon should he have one.

OPTIONAL TECHNIQUES

Passing the Guard - 3, 39, 40, 41, 44, 45, 58

CLINCH AND TAKEDOWN —
OFFENSE AND DEFENSE

In this section, you get the basics of clinching and takedowns so you can choose where you want the fight to take place, whether standing or on the ground. Clinching is the fork on the road; if you want to take your opponent down you will need to clinch him, but if you don't want to be taken to the ground, you need to know the basics of how to counter his clinch and takedown attempts. In many combat situations, you may not want to go to the ground, or be in the bottom position, due to a two on one attack or because the ground surface may contain hazards like rocks, shrapnel or glass. The ability to defend a takedown and execute a proper takedown will give you the tools to make that decision and conduct the fight in the element that you choose.

NECK GRAB

Aitor sneaks up behind Greg and grabs his neck in an attempt to choke him. Greg's quick reaction with the proper technique will save his life.

1 Aitor sneaks up from behind and grabs Greg's neck with his left arm for a rear choke. Greg's first concerns are to protect his neck and then maintain his base so he doesn't get taken down to the ground. He first cups both hands over Aitor's left forearm and pulls the forearm down by bringing his elbows down and next to his side. He then drops in base by opening the legs out slightly wider than his shoulders, bending the knees, pushing his buttocks back and maintaining a straight line between his back and head. It is important for Greg's hips to be below Aitor's hips and pushing back.

2 Greg explosively extends his legs as he drops his head down towards the ground while still keeping his back straight, sending Aitor flying over his head. Greg steps back with the right leg, keeps control over Aitor's left arm by pulling it up so he can't roll away and delivers a kick to the head with the right leg.

OVER THE ARMS CLINCH

Another common clinch from the rear is the over the arms clinch. Again, quick reaction and proper technique will yield positive results so it is important to practice these diligently until you automatically react properly to any grab.

1 Aitor gets a rear clinch over Greg's arms. Greg drops in base, opens his elbows out slightly and grabs over Aitor's hands with his hands. Greg pushes off his feet, extending his body, and delivers a head butt to Aitor's face.

2 He then steps out with his right foot, swings the left leg around Aitor's right leg so his hips are perpendicular to Aitor's hips and his left thigh pushes against the back of Aitor's left thigh. Greg reaches with both hands and grabs the back of Aitor's knees – the right hand grabs the back of the right knee and the left hand (passing in front of Aitor's legs) grabs the back of the left knee.

3 Greg pushes off his legs and turns his shoulders in a counter-clockwise direction, heaving Aitor over his hip as if he were throwing a sack of cement. As Aitor falls to the ground, Greg places his right shin against Aitor's left side, ready to strike him with a punch or a kick.

H2H
TECHNIQUE 074
CLINCH AND TAKEDOWN — OFFENSE AND DEFENSE

UNDER THE ARMS CLINCH

This time, Aitor clinches Greg under the arms. It is important for Greg to see which of Aitor's hands is on top as he will attack that arm to break the grip.

1 Aitor clinches Greg from the rear. His left hand grabs over the right so Greg will attack that hand. Greg pushes Aitor's left wrist with both hands as he drops down in base. Greg then grabs Aitor's left index finger with his left hand and pulls it back, forcing Aitor to give up the grip or break his finger.

2 Greg then steps forward and out with the right foot while still controlling Aitor's left arm by the wrist. He takes a step around Aitor's right leg with his left leg, with the foot landing next to and outside of Aitor's right foot. Greg wraps the left arm around Aitor's back until he can grab the left hip with his hand. Greg delivers a right knee to Aitor's stomach as he pushes off his right foot and pulls Aitor's left arm, adding to the strength of the blow.

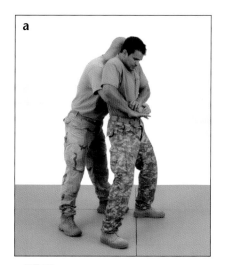

a

b

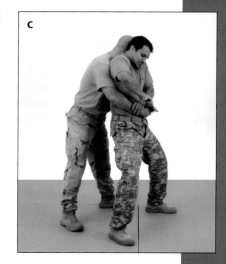

c

3 Alternatively, if he has a knife, Greg can use it to escape the grab and cut his enemy. He attacks the arm on the same side of his weapon, in this case the right side. Greg grabs Aitor's right wrist with his hands to prevent him from using it to grab his knife. He then reaches and pulls his knife with the right hand and slices Aitor on the tendon in his hand.

4 Aitor breaks his grip in reaction to the stab. Greg steps around to his right while holding Aitor's left arm open.

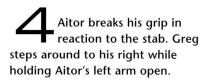

5 Greg can slash the throat as he swings his arm back, or stab the right side of Aitor's neck with the knife and pull it back to stab the chest.

REAR CHOKE

Being able to quickly and effectively render your enemy unconscious is an extremely important tool in the field and in a fight. With the rear choke, you can choose whether to just make him unconscious, or in extreme cases (as in battle), to kill him by holding the choke longer.

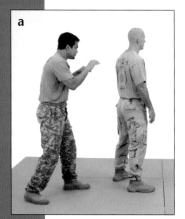
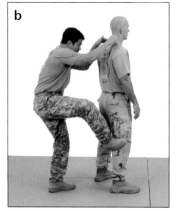

1 Greg approaches Aitor from the back. He grabs his shoulders with both hands and pulls them back as he strikes the back of his right leg with the bottom of his right foot, forcing him to bend backwards. Always choke with the left arm so you can transition to your weapon with the right hand.

2 Greg wraps his left arm around Aitor's neck, making sure his elbow is centered and in front of the Adam's apple, and his left hand reaches Aitor's right shoulder. Greg bends the right arm and grabs his own right biceps with his left hand. Greg slides his right hand behind Aitor's head and applies the choke by bringing his elbows together and pulling them into his own chest while driving his head forward against the back of Aitor's head. Greg pushes his left knee against Aitor's coccyx to prevent him from straightening his body.

OPTIONAL TECHNIQUES

18, 76, 77

ANATOMY OF TECHNIQUES

K) Blood flow (Arteries)

VARIATION

The same choke can be applied if the opponent falls backwards. Make sure to place the heels of your feet on his hips to control them and prevent him from escaping.

REAR CHOKE FROM CLINCH

The rear choke can be very effective from a rear clinch. By using the element of surprise just as you drop the enemy down after hoisting him up, you can quickly sink in the rear choke.

1 Greg has a rear clinch on Aitor with his arms wrapped around the waist, hands locked in front and trapping Aitor's left wrist. Greg presses his left knee forward against Aitor's coccyx, forcing him to bend back, and pushes off his legs to lift Aitor off the ground. Notice that Greg uses his legs and hips to hoist Aitor up and back, causing his legs to swing forward. When Greg drops him back to the ground, Aitor's legs are out and his body is falling back.

2 Greg steps forward with his left leg, again pressing the knee on Aitor's coccyx. He quickly wraps his left arm around the neck and applies the rear choke as he grabs his right biceps with the left hand, bends the right arm, inserts the hand behind Aitor's head and brings his elbows together, applying the choking pressure. Always choke with the left arm so you can transition to your weapon with the right hand.

OPTIONAL TECHNIQUES

18, 75, 77

ANATOMY OF TECHNIQUES

K) Blood flow (Arteries)

REAR SUPERMAN DUMP

The rear superman dump is a great takedown when you can surprise and attack the opponent from the rear. The key to this takedown is to grab below the opponent's knees and drive your shoulders forward against his thighs or hips, forcing his body to fall forward as his feet are taken from under him.

1 Greg sneaks from behind his opponent and crouches down and lunges forward, taking a big step with his left leg so his foot lands between Peter's feet. At the same time, Greg grabs Peter's legs just under the knees. Greg's shoulders are aimed to hit right at Peter's buttocks.

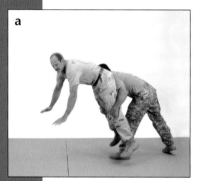
a

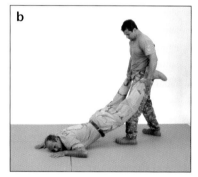
b

c

2 Greg pushes off his legs as he raises his body, pushing the shoulder against Peter's buttocks and pulling the legs back with his hands, forcing Peter to fall forward and on his face. Notice that Greg purposely lifts Peter's legs up so Peter falls hard on his face. Greg kicks Peter in the groin with his right leg.

3 Greg takes advantage of Peter being stunned from the impact of the fall and the groin strike to get the rear mount and apply the rear choke. Greg can also deliver a series of blows to the face and back of the head before he chokes Peter.

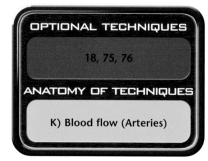

OPTIONAL TECHNIQUES
18, 75, 76

ANATOMY OF TECHNIQUES
K) Blood flow (Arteries)

SPRAWLING LOW SHOOT COUNTER

Sprawling is a very efficient way to counter a single or double leg takedown. In this case, Aitor shoots low, trying to take control over Greg's legs and take him down. Greg sprawls and breaks Aitor's control.

1 Aitor shoots low for a double leg take-down. Greg counters it by sprawling as he shoots his legs back, planting the feet wider than his shoulders and pressing the hips down while keeping the legs straight. Greg then pivots off his feet and turns his shoulders and hips counter-clockwise, further deflecting Aitor's power. Greg wraps his left arm in front of Aitor's left side of the face, reaching with his left hand and grabbing Aitor's right triceps to force his face back.

2 As an alternative counter to the shoot, Greg sprawls and pushes on the back of Aitor's head, forcing it down.

DOUBLE-LEG TAKEDOWN

The double-leg takedown is one of the favorite takedowns for wrestlers, MMA fighters and fighters in field combat situations. In the double-leg, you quickly secure control over the opponent's legs and use an explosive thrust from the legs to drive back the shoulders on the opponent's midsection, causing him to fall down.

1 Greg and Aitor face each other. Both are in orthodox fighting stances with their left feet forward. Greg bends his knees, dropping his body down, while his hands are in front of his face to protect it from any strikes as he readies to lunge forward for the tackle. Greg pushes off his right foot and shoots forward with his shoulders aimed at the front of Aitor's thighs and his hands wrapping the back of the thighs.

OPTIONAL TECHNIQUES

17, 47, 51, 80, 81, 87

2 Greg drops his left knee to the ground and in between Aitor's legs. Greg wants to kneel closer to Aitor's forward leg as he wraps both hands behind Aitor's thighs. Greg's chest presses tightly against Aitor's legs and his head pushes against the right side of the ribs. Greg steps forward with the right leg, hooking the foot behind Aitor's left foot as he drives his shoulders forward, pressing them against Aitor's thighs.

3 Greg continues to move forward and drive his shoulders against Aitor's hips. Since he cannot step back to regain his balance, Aitor falls back to the ground.

DOUBLE-LEG TAKEDOWN:
Opponent counters

Many times, when you shoot for a double-leg takedown, a smart opponent will counter by sprawling as he shoots his legs back and forces his hips forward, stopping the takedown motion. In that case, use this alternative.

a

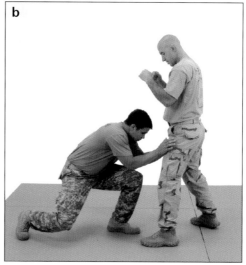

b

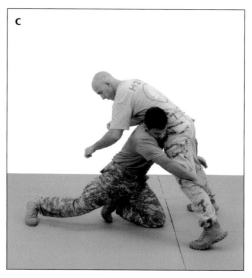

c

1 Greg and Aitor face each other. Greg shoots forward, attempting a double-leg takedown. Aitor counters it by shooting his legs back and sprawling. Although Greg's hands reach the back of Aitor's thighs, he doesn't have enough control to succeed in the double-leg.

OPTIONAL TECHNIQUES

17, 47, 51, 79, 81, 87

2 Greg steps forward with the right leg to cut the distance between his hips and Aitor's hips. He is now able to better secure his control over Aitor's legs. Notice that at this point Greg's shoulders are under Aitor's hips and Aitor's head and torso are leaning far forward, making his legs very light. Greg pushes his head to the left, pressing it against Aitor's left side, and pulls the legs out to the right, taking Aitor down to the ground.

STANDING DROP: *Outside trip*

Many times, when you clinch an opponent and set up for a takedown, he tries to pull away. There are several options to take advantage of his reaction, some previously addressed in this book; the outside trip is another solid effective option to take your opponent to the ground. The outside trip works anytime you are able to clinch and your opponent leans away. It does not need to be used in combination with techniques like the hip throw and can be your first option.

1 Greg clinches Peter and sets up the hip throw. Peter tries to escape and defend as he leans to his left. Greg drops his body down. He presses his head against Peter's stomach and hooks his left leg around the back of Peter's right leg as he grabs Peter's left knee with his right hand. Note that Greg locks his foot right next to Peter's right foot and his calf presses against the back of Peter's calf to prevent him from stepping away.

OPTIONAL TECHNIQUES

17, 47, 51, 79, 80, 87

2 Greg drops to his left knee and extends his body by pushing the hips forward, driving his head and chest against Peter's side while grabbing the back of the knees with his hands. At the same time, he pulls his left leg back, sweeping Peter's right foot off the ground and forcing him to fall to his back.

3 Greg maintains control over Peter's legs with his chest, pinning them down and pushing them in with his arms. Greg crawls over the legs and ends up mounted on Peter.

ARM DRAG

The arm drag is a very effective way to secure an advantage and take your opponent's back from the over-under clinch. The key to the arm drag is to get your opponent to commit his weight forward and then quickly pull his arm across the body.

1 Greg and Aitor are clinched in the standard over-under clinch. Greg slides his right hand back along Aitor's left arm until he reaches and grabs Aitor's left wrist.

OPTIONAL TECHNIQUES

17, 47, 51, 79, 80, 81, 87

2 Greg pushes the wrist down and across his body, forcing Aitor to turn to his right, exposing his back. With his left hand, Greg grabs Aitor's left triceps and pulls the arm forward as he steps forward with his right leg and slides to Aitor's back. Greg wraps his arms around Aitor's torso for control. His right hand still holds Aitor's left wrist and his left hand grabs the left arm at the biceps.

REVERSE

2 Notice how Greg grabs Aitor's left wrist with the right hand and the back of the arm at the triceps with the left hand, setting up the arm drag. Greg pulls the arm across his body so he can go to the back.

GETTING THE CLINCH

Being able to counter a clinch from your enemy is very important and Greg has already demonstrated a few counters to common clinches. Now he will show how to clinch the opponent and reach an advantageous position.

 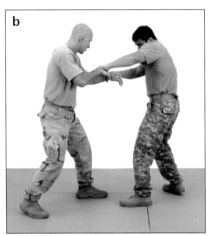 

1 Greg and Aitor face each other in a fight. Each has his left foot forward and the hands out ready to attack. Greg places both hands on top of Aitor's hands and pulls them out, allowing him to break inside Aitor's strike distance without fear of a punch. Since Greg had his left foot forward he leads with the left forearm so it can block the punch. If the punch goes down the middle it will hit Greg's elbow.

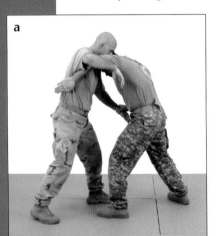 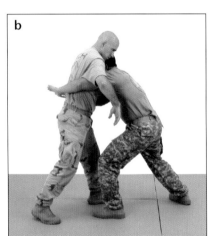 

2 While still holding Aitor's left wrist open, Greg bends the knees, dropping his body down and reaching with his left arm under Aitor's right armpit. He then lets go of the grip on Aitor's left wrist and wraps his right arm under Aitor's left armpit until he can lock his hands behind the back. Greg pulls his hands in and drives his head and chest up against Aitor's chest, securing the clinch.

OPTIONAL TECHNIQUES

84, 85

H2H
TECHNIQUE
084

RHINO CLINCH

If the opponents start throwing punches, the rhino clinch is a great way to clinch and connect while avoiding the punches.

OPTIONAL TECHNIQUES

83, 85

1 Greg and Aitor face each other in a fight, each with his left foot forward and the hands out ready to attack. Aitor tries a left jab and Greg parries it down with his right hand, circling down and grabbing over the wrist. Greg places his left hand to the top left of his head so his elbow points forward and the arm acts as a block to Aitor's right punches. Notice that Greg's left arm is in the shape of the horn of a rhino.

  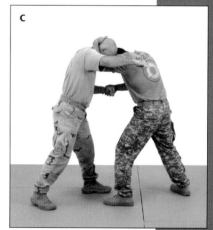

2 Greg steps forward with his left foot, cutting the distance between himself and Aitor. Greg leads with the left elbow, his arm still covering his face. Aitor throws a right punch but Greg slips it as he is too close to Aitor. Greg then reaches and grabs the back of Aitor's head with his left hand while still controlling the left wrist with his right hand. Greg could then go for a Thai clinch, locking both hands behind Aitor's neck.

H2H TECHNIQUE 085

SLIP UNDER CLINCH

One of the best opportunities to clinch in a combat or street fight situation is when your opponent initiates a strike. By timing your clinching attempt properly, you can either cut the distance early before your opponent's strike reaches its range of power or, as in this case, simply slip under the punch and clinch. Remember, it is imperative that you control your anxiety to clinch and instead concentrate on slipping the punch first so you avoid getting hit and perhaps being knocked out!

1 Aitor throws a left jab. Greg ducks the punch by bending his knees and dropping his torso down and to his right. At the same time, he leans forward and parries the jab with his right hand, striking the back of Aitor's forearm and pushing it from right to left.

REVERSE

1 Notice how Greg's arm and head position protect his face from strikes. Greg tucks his chin down until it almost touches his chest. He holds both arms bent at the elbow. The right forearm aims up with the palm of the hand facing forward and right in front of his face, protecting against any straight punches. The left forearm points slightly down, with the palm of the hand facing out and the shoulder tight against the left side of the face. The shoulder protects the face from any right crosses while the hand is ready to parry punches.

2 Greg's strike on the back of Aitor's left arm forces Aitor's torso to turn, exposing his back. Greg pushes off his back foot (here, his right foot) to cut the distance and drives his head next to Aitor's left arm until it touches his left side. Greg then wraps his arms around Aitor's torso, locking his palms together as he pushes his head against the left shoulder. Greg keeps his head tight against the shoulder to prevent Aitor from bringing his left arm in front of Greg's head and gaining a neutral clinch. As it is, Greg has the advantage.

OPTIONAL TECHNIQUES

83, 84

STANDING ARM TRIANGLE CHOKE

Any time you are able to segregate your opponent's head and arm to one side with your arm, you can attempt this head and arm choke. Here Greg demonstrates the standing version of the choke, but the same choke can be used effectively from the side mount, the half-guard and other positions. Be on the lookout for opportunities to use this choke. This technique can also be done from side control and the mount. Always have your head on the weapon side.

1 Greg ducks under Aitor's left hook and slips his left arm on the right side of his neck. As he raises his body, Greg drives his head up and under Aitor's left armpit, pushing it against the left shoulder so as to trap the left arm.

2 Greg wraps the left arm tightly around Aitor's head, reaching with his hand until he can grab his own right biceps. Greg uses his right hand to push Aitor's forehead and applies the choke by bringing his elbows together and back, cinching the noose around Aitor's neck and arm.

REVERSE

2 Notice how Greg's left arm wraps around the right side of Aitor's head and how he uses his head to push Aitor's left arm in. Greg's right hand pushing against Aitor's forehead helps him pull his elbows tight to secure the choke.

ANATOMY OF TECHNIQUES

K) Blood flow (Arteries)

STANDING ARM TRIANGLE, TAKEDOWN, TRANSITION

Greg here demonstrates a great transition from the head clinch to the arm choke and takedown. Notice how he snaps Aitor's head down and quickly ducks under the arm to connect the choke before he goes for a takedown transition.

1 Greg has Aitor in a head clinch with his hands cupping the back of his head and neck. His elbows are close together to secure the hold. In a sudden move, Greg snaps Aitor's head down and he releases it upon his reaction and ducks under the left arm. At the same time, Greg shoots his left arm over Aitor's right shoulder near the neck.

2 Greg drives his head against Aitor's left shoulder, trapping the arm. He wraps the left arm around the neck until he can clasp his hands together, palm to palm. Greg applies the choke by pulling his left hand in with the right and pushing his head against Aitor's left arm in the arm choke fashion explained previously.

3 Switching angles to view the takedown, Greg pivots off his left foot so his hips are aligned with Aitor's hips. He swings his right leg in, striking the back of Aitor's left thigh with his right knee, causing the leg to buckle.

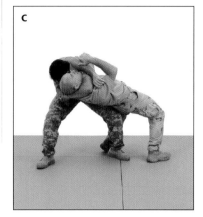

4 Greg opens his hips so he can swing the left leg around Aitor's left leg and plant the foot between Aitor's feet. Greg's left thigh and hip are firmly set behind Aitor's left thigh. He twists his shoulders to his right (clockwise), forcing Aitor to fall to the ground. Greg controls the takedown as he wants to maintain his choke. He ends up on the ground next to Aitor's left side with the choke still secured and applies extra pressure as he drops his hips down, pushes off his feet and drives his shoulder and head against Aitor's arm and neck.

SIDE VIEW

4 Check out Greg's body position: hips pressing down, left arm and head surrounding Aitor's head and arm for the choke.

5 Alternatively, Greg may choose to reach for his knife or gun with his free hand as he secures the arm choke position.

OPTIONAL TECHNIQUES

17, 47, 51, 79, 80, 81

GUILLOTINE FLOW DRILL

Note: For weapon retention, Aitor's head is on the left so that Greg can transition to a weapon or prevent Aitor from grabbing it. If Greg did not have a weapon and was concerned about Aitor transitioning to a weapon, he would have Aitor's head under his right arm. Number one rule in a clinch: Always keep your head on the weapon side.

This is a great drill to develop your use of the guillotine when your opponent attempts a double leg or single leg takedown, or after knees in Thai clinch.

1 Greg has a head clinch on Aitor. Aitor shoots in for a double leg takedown.

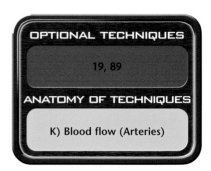

OPTIONAL TECHNIQUES

19, 89

ANATOMY OF TECHNIQUES

K) Blood flow (Arteries)

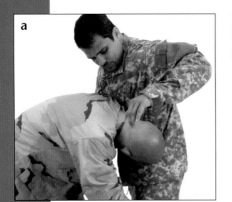

a

b

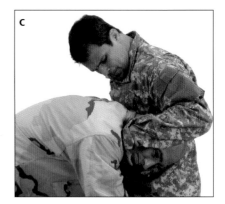

c

2 Greg wraps the left arm around Aitor's neck and uses his hand to pull Aitor's chin up, exposing the neck. Greg's armpit should be on the top of Aitor's head and holding it like a football. This will make it hard for Aitor to slip out or lift Greg up.

a

b

c

d

3 Reversing the angle for best view: Greg grabs his own collar with the right hand and dips his right shoulder, giving it to the left so he can tighten the grip around Aitor's neck. He then wraps his right arm under Aitor's left arm and drives it up, which helps with weapon retention, as he turns his torso to the right and looks while shrugging his right shoulder up to choke him.

e

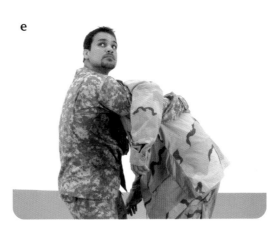

STANDING CRUCIFIX

Continuing with the drill from the Cloth guillotine, Greg changes to the standing crucifix.

1 Greg has his right arm under Aitor's left arm while his left elbow presses down on the back of the head to keep Aitor from raising it and gaining posture.

2 Greg slips his left arm under Aitor's right arm and locks his hands together behind Aitor's back. Greg uses his chest to press down on Aitor's head, applying the pressure of the crucifix to the back of the neck.

3 If you can't reach around to lock up your hands because your opponent is too large, then roll up the cloth of his shirt or jacket, bunching it up so you can get a solid grip. Notice how Greg curls all his fingers under the cloth to secure the best grip.

INCORRECT

3 Greg doesn't insert the fingers under the bunched cloth. This results in a weaker grip and when Aitor tries to escape, Greg's hands slip down and he loses the grip.

4 Options from the crucifix: Greg can choose to knee Aitor to the head.

5 Or he can go back to the guillotine.

OPTIONAL TECHNIQUES

19, 88

a

b

c

d

6 Or he can switch the control grip and use his left hand to push down on the back of Aitor's head, and then deliver a knee strike to the head from the side with his left knee.

H2H TECHNIQUE 090

SPINNING IN CLINCH

As previously stated, it may be advantageous to spin your opponent and throw him against an object such as a wall, a post, a vehicle or other opponents. Here, Greg demonstrates a great way to spin the opponent during an over-under clinch. The key to the move is to always spin towards the front foot and use both pressure on that same side shoulder and your opponent's reaction to assist you in spinning him.

1 Greg and Aitor are clinched with the over-under grip. Greg has his head on the left side of Aitor's head, the left arm under Aitor's right armpit and his right arm over Aitor's left arm, gripping the elbow. Aitor has a similar grip on Greg. Greg wants to spin Aitor. Since his left foot is forward, Greg will spin him over that foot. He begins the move by driving his right shoulder forward against Aitor's left shoulder. Aitor reacts by pushing back with the left shoulder. Greg steps back and to the left of center line with the right foot and pulls down on Aitor's left arm with his right hand while driving his left arm forward and up, pushing Aitor's shoulders in a clockwise direction.

2 Greg continues to push Aitor's left elbow down and push his right arm up while circling his right back towards his left, forcing Aitor to spin around his left leg and end up at 180° from where he started.

VARIATION

2 Greg may step on Aitor's left foot with his right foot to prevent him from moving it and regaining his balance in an attempt to counter the spin.

SPINNING IN THAI CLINCH

If you are locked in a Thai clinch, the spinning technique is slightly different, as demonstrated here. In this case, you'll take advantage of the fact that you have control over the enemy's head to help turn him.

1 Greg has Aitor's head locked in a Thai clinch with his hand locked behind the head and the elbows tight against the side of the face, forming a cage around the head. Greg uses his control over Aitor's head to turn him as Greg first steps back and to his left of center line with the right foot, turning Aitor's head to his right by raising both elbows up towards the right. The pressure on Aitor's head forces him to turn and the body soon to follow.

 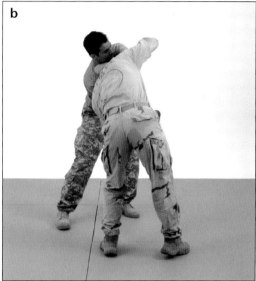

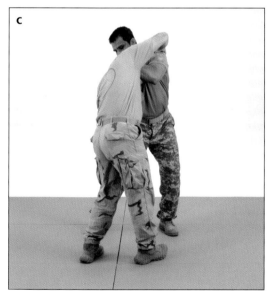 

2 Greg then pulls Aitor's head down and forward, forcing him to step forward with the right leg to maintain his balance. Greg then immediately turns his torso and his elbows in a clockwise direction, forcing Aitor's head to swing up to the left and forcing him to step around with the right leg and be spun until he ends up 180° from where he started.

THAI CLINCH COUNTER

A very common and dangerous clinch used in combat and street fights is the Thai clinch. In the Thai clinch, the opponent uses his hands on the back of your head and pulls it down while pressing his elbows in so his forearms frame and trap your head, preventing it from moving. From the Thai clinch, the attacker can deliver powerful knee strikes to your face as he drives the knees up while pulling your head down into the strike. Therefore it is very important to be able to effectively counter the Thai clinch.

1 Aitor has Greg in a Thai clinch with his hands cupping the back of Greg's head and the elbows pressing in, locking Greg's head in place. Greg circles his left hand under Aitor's right arm, inserting the hand just above the elbow until he can grip the back of Aitor's neck.

2 Greg repeats the motion on the opposite side, using his right hand to grab Aitor's head and reverse the control.

REVERSE

2 Notice how Greg drops his right shoulder down, making it easier to circle the hand under Aitor's arm, and shoots the hand up right between their heads, breaking the control and then gripping the back of the head.

THAI CLINCH COUNTER AND SWEEP

A great counter to the Thai clinch is shown here. In it, Greg alters the normal counter and goes for a sweep.

1 Aitor has Greg in a Thai clinch. Greg's hands grab Aitor's forearms, pulling them open to try to break the clinch. Greg starts his counter by grabbing the outside of Aitor's right elbow with his right hand and pulling it across his body. He then loops his left hand over Aitor's right shoulder.

2 Greg reaches around Aitor's back and grabs the left armpit or neck. Notice that Aitor is off-balance as Greg is twisting him to the right. Greg then swings his left leg around and kicks Aitor's left leg in with his right foot for the takedown.

CONTROL OF FIXED OBJECTS

It is extremely important to be aware of your surroundings and take advantage of any fixed objects you can use to inflict damage and control your opponent. Always turn your opponent into a fixed object (walls, chairs, doors, etc.) with the intent of slamming and hurting him. Push with controlled force, if possible, so the impact will take some of the fight out of him. Most importantly, use the fixed object to assist in controlling him and his escape routes.

Note: If your opponent does not have a good foundation, you can simply circle him and push him where you want him.

1 Greg and Aitor are in a neutral over-under clinch. Greg is aware of the wall behind him and wants to take advantage of it.

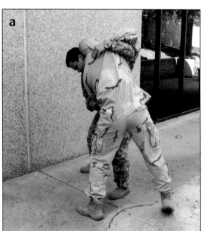

2 Greg pushes into Aitor so Aitor will push back. This is needed to help with the spin. Greg takes a quick step to his right with his left foot, immediately followed by a step back and to his left with the right foot. At the same time, he pulls Aitor's left elbow down and right elbow up in a circular motion while stepping slightly to the left, spinning him and using his forward pressure to throw him against the wall. Greg pins Aitor to the wall by pressing his shoulders and chest against Aitor's chest. Greg's right hand still controls Aitor's left elbow while his left arm is positioned under Aitor's right armpit.

3 Greg delivers a right knee strike to Aitor's groin, forcing him to raise his right leg to protect his groin from another knee strike. Greg hooks his left leg around Aitor's right leg and pulls it first back and then counter-clockwise, forcing Aitor to fall to the ground. Greg puts his right knee on Aitor's stomach, presses his right hand on Aitor's left shoulder to prevent him from getting back up, and cocks his left hand, ready to strike.

H2H

TECHNIQUE
095

MORE OBJECTS

At times, you may find yourself in a bad situation, with your enemy pushing you against an immobile object such as a wall or a bench. You need to use cunning to escape the pin and take advantage of your opponent's body position to spin him around and not only escape but reverse the situation and pin him against the object.

1 Aitor pins Greg against the wall. They both have an over-under clinch stance with Aitor's head on Greg's left side.

2 Since Aitor's head is on his left side, Greg wants to spin him to his right, away from the head. Greg first pushes his left shoulder against Aitor's right as if he wanted to turn to his left and escape the wall. Aitor naturally counters the push with a push of his own as he drives his weight and pressure to his left shoulder. Greg quickly steps to his left with his left foot, then the right one as he turns his shoulders to the right while pulling Aitor's left arm with the right hand and spins Aitor into the wall, reversing the situation.

WEAPON TRANSITIONS, TAKEAWAYS, AND BASIC KNIFE

Transition leverage: Weapon control and retention:

In a CQB environment, ultimately the winner of the fight is the person who controls the weapon. In Weapon Transitions and Takeaways you will learn some of the most effective, battle proven techniques to control a situation. You will learn to maintain control of your weapon and how to take away your enemy's weapon, be that a knife, gun or rifle. You will also learn how to transition to your secondary weapon should your primary weapon become too cumbersome to maneuver and effectively be used (such as a rifle in a clinch) or if it fails to operate (such as a pistol with a round stuck in the chamber).

When weapons are introduced in a confrontation, everything changes. The first and main objective should always be control: take away or retain the weapon. Retaining your weapon is vital to survival in a dynamic close quarter combat situation. If you and your enemy hit the ground, you need to get to a side mount or mount for leverage. If your enemy gets you in the guard, you do not have as much leverage to take away or keep the weapon. This is one of the reasons to train in grappling. Grapplers are weapon transition experts and do not always know it. The instinct to gravitate to a leverage position is priceless. From a mount or side mount you can use your weight to pin and control the enemy's weapon hand, as demonstrated here.

FRONT CLINCH

The common front clinch, with both hands controlling the upper body, is easily foiled using a stiff arm or using your arms as a frame.

1 Aitor tries to grab Greg from the front with both arms open. Greg steps back with his right foot and places his hands on Aitor's shoulders with both arms extended, blocking Aitor from grabbing him.

2 Should Greg be slightly slow and unable to get his arms extended in time, he can make a frame with his left forearm in front of Aitor's throat. The right hand grips the left wrist to complete the frame.

ANATOMY OF TECHNIQUES

J) Torso

REVERSE

2 Check out Greg's frame: his left forearm is in front of Aitor's throat. The right hand gripping the left wrist completes the frame.

LEFT SIDE CLINCH

As Aitor approaches Greg from the left, Greg's first concern is to gain base and then block the grab. Note: you may want to practice this in kit (body armor) and/or with a rifle.

a

b

c

1 Greg is standing with his feet shoulder width apart. When Aitor attacks from the left side, Greg turns to his left, bends his knees so as to have better base, and bends his arms so as to form a frame, with the left forearm facing forward and the right hand grabbing the left wrist. Greg thrusts the left forearm against Aitor's throat.

2 If Greg has a knife in a field combat situation, after stopping Aitor's momentum, Greg releases the grip on his left wrist and uses the right hand to draw the knife and stab Aitor.

RIGHT SIDE GRAB

When Aitor approaches Greg from the right side (where his weapon is), in addition to being in base as before, Greg needs to change blocking hands to use the weapon. Note: again, you may want to practice this in kit and/or with a rifle.

1 Aitor tries to grab Greg from the right side. Greg turns to his right and bends at the knees to get in base. He leans forward on his right leg and makes a frame with his right hand on Aitor's right shoulder and the forearm blocking his throat. Greg uses his left hand to grab his right wrist to support the frame.

2 Because his knife is on his right side, Greg moves his left forearm to block Aitor's throat as he releases his grip on the right wrist and places the left hand on Aitor's right shoulder. Now Greg has his forearm in an X in front of Aitor's throat and he can switch his base as he steps back with his right foot and forward with the left. Greg reaches with his right hand, grabs his knife and stabs Aitor on the stomach.

REVERSE

2 Notice Greg's left hand position on Aitor's left shoulder: he cups his hand over the shoulder to give him a brace so his forearm presses against Aitor's throat and blocks him from moving forward and cutting the distance. Greg can stab him with the knife.

H2H
TECHNIQUE
099

OVER THE ARMS

One common clinch is the front grab over the arms, also known as a bear hug. In the bear hug the opponent not only wraps his arms over your arms but also tries to pull your spine and squeeze you. This can be very uncomfortable and even dangerous if you are faced with a very strong opponent.

Note: For weapon transition, retention and take away, it is crucial to get your head on the weapon side for leverage. If your enemy gets your head on the opposite side, you will not have as much leverage to take away or keep the weapon. It is vital that you make this an instinctive movement.

Counters to clinch:

At times you are not fast enough or aware enough to react to the clinch attempt and block it before it is complete so it is very important to know how to escape from the completed clinch as well.

1 Aitor grabs Greg over his arms in a common bear hug. Greg's first concern is to create some space so Aitor cannot pull him too tight and injure him. Greg places his hands on Aitor's hips, bracing against them and keeping them in place. Greg drops in base as he bends his knees. He steps back with the right leg, creating space between their hips.

a

b

If Greg's head is on the left side of Aitor's head, Greg can bite Aitor's throat or shirt-covered shoulder, forcing Aitor to pull back so Greg can switch his head to the right side so Greg can have leverage over the weapon before introducing it to the fight.

c

COUNTER TO CLINCH: *Under arms*

In this case, Aitor bear hugs under the arms, controlling Greg's mid-section. The person with the inside control always has an advantage in a clinching situation and can take Greg down. Greg first has to deal with being in base, creating space and, finally pummeling, so he can have the inside control.

1 Aitor clinches Greg around his waist in a bear hug under the arms. With his arms controlling the inside, Aitor has a definite advantage in the clinch battle over Greg. Greg quickly counters by dropping in base and leaning forward with his weight. It is important for Greg to have his weight forward so he can use his chest, pushing it against Aitor's chest to counter Aitor's forward pressure and maintain his balance. He takes a step back with his right leg and bends his left leg so his weight is forward and his hips are away from Aitor's hips. Greg evens the clinch control by wrapping his arms tightly around Aitor's arms above the elbows. Greg clinches his palms together to secure the grip.

2 Having stopped Aitor's initial attack and control, Greg now concentrates on gaining control of the inside himself. He turns his shoulder to the left and coils his left arm back so he can slide his hand inside Aitor's right arm near the shoulder. Notice that Greg has his palm facing in, with the fingers extended together so they can easily slip in the space created by his torso turning. Greg drives his left arm all the way through until he can wrap the arm around Aitor's right shoulder controlling the back.

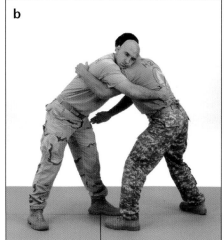

3 Greg repeats the motion to the right side as he turns his shoulders to the right, inserting his right arm inside and wrapping it around Aitor's back. Greg grabs his hands together, cinching the grip on the back. Greg drops his body down, bending the knees, ready to take Aitor down.

REVERSE

4 Notice, since Greg's head is on Aitor's right, Greg's turning his torso to the right creates space between his chest and Aitor's left arm at the elbow and not at the shoulder level as was the case when he turned to his left.

WEAPON RENTENTION KNEE RAKE

In this case, while escaping the bear hug under the arms, Greg has a knife on his right side and is ready to use it when Aitor grabs his wrist, blocking the strike. The same technique can be used to release the wrist from a grip when holding a pistol or any other weapon.

1 Greg escapes Aitor's bear hug as he pummels the right side, which puts Greg's head on the weapon side, giving him better control. Greg reaches for his knife with the right hand and is ready to stab Aitor. Aitor grabs Greg's right wrist with his left hand, blocking the attack.

2 Greg coils his right leg up so he can drive his knee over his wrist and Aitor's hand. His shin acts as a block. Greg turns his torso to the right as he extends his right leg forward, the shin pushing against Aitor's left forearm. He pulls his right arm back, breaking Aitor's grip and freeing his hand. Greg stabs Aitor with his knife with an outside strike of his right hand.

REAR GRAB: *Go to knife*

In case of the rear grab, Greg's first concern is to maintain control of his pistol and then transition to the knife attack.

1 Greg is attacked from the rear. Aitor wraps his left arm around the neck and uses his right hand to try to pry away Greg's gun. Greg grabs Aitor's right hand with his own right hand, pushing down on the hand to prevent Aitor from pulling the gun out of the holster. Since Aitor comes in with the left arm to choke, Greg looks to his right and tucks his chin in tight against his chest. He then grabs Aitor's left wrist with his left hand and pulls it down, preventing the choke.

2 Greg then quickly releases his grip on Aitor's left arm and reaches for his knife with the left hand, pulling it out and stabbing Aitor's left thigh with it. Notice that at all times Greg keeps pressing down with his right hand on the pistol.

3 The stab at the leg causes Aitor to step back with his left leg. Greg pivots off his right foot and steps out with his left leg so he faces Aitor. Greg then circles his knife in, slashing Aitor's right hand and forcing him to release the grip on the pistol. Greg then is able to draw the pistol and point or shoot at Aitor.

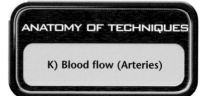

ANATOMY OF TECHNIQUES

K) Blood flow (Arteries)

SHOULDER LOCK

In this front grab, Aitor tries to tackle Greg. Greg makes sure Aitor's head is away from his weapon side and blocks his weapon before he goes for the lock.

1 Aitor tries to clinch Greg from the front. Greg blocks his attempt by bracing with his left forearm against Aitor's neck, preventing him from getting his pistol by controlling the left wrist with his right hand. Greg then quickly wraps his left arm around Aitor's left arm until his left hand locks with his right wrist, securing the figure 4 lock on the arm.

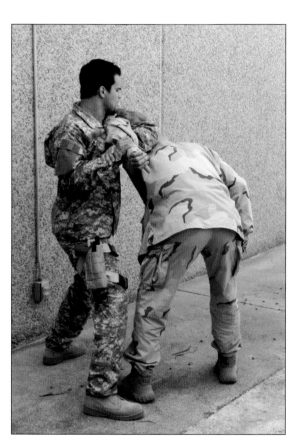

2 Greg steps to his right and torques Aitor's left arm around the shoulder for the shoulder lock. Greg takes advantage of a nearby wall (he could use another large object if a wall is not available) as he pushes off his right leg while still torquing the arm, driving Aitor's head into the wall.

OPTIONAL TECHNIQUES

19, 88, 89

TWO-HANDED WEAPON RETENTION

Many times the enemy comes at you with both hands to get your weapon. Use these solid moves to stop and strike him.

1 Peter comes in and tries to grab Greg's gun with both hands. Greg places his left forearm in front of Peter's chest and between his arms with the hand grabbing the left biceps to stop his advance. His right hand pushes down on Peter's hands to prevent him from drawing the gun. Since Peter's head is on the weapon side, and Greg is unable to get his head on the weapon side, Greg bites the right side of Peter's neck, forcing him to retreat slightly and allowing Greg to move his head in front of Peter's head, blocking the sight of the gun and gaining leverage of the weapon. Note: Because of Aids and hepatitis, biting can be very dangerous. Make sure you have no other options. Also, remember that it is safer to bite over clothing.

a

b

2 Greg pivots to his right, and keeps his right hand on top of Peter's hands. He then steps in front of Peter with his left leg, planting the toe of the foot just in front of Peter's outside foot. Greg puts his hip outside of Peter's left hip and continues to twist his body to his right, applying a hip throw and sending Peter to the ground.

c

ALTERNATIVE

3 Alternatively, Greg may be able to push Peter away with his left arm and maintain distance and control over his weapon.

OPTIONAL TECHNIQUES

111

SIDE CONTROL: *Mount and guard with pistol*

Greg demonstrates here why you shouldn't transition to your weapon when your opponent has side control or the mount on you. See how easily Peter can counter and control the weapon.

From side control:

Peter has side control on Greg. Greg reaches for his pistol with his right hand. This is not a very safe position to introduce a weapon. Peter immediately transitions to control the pistol: with both hands open and arms bent, Peter wants to grab and pin Greg's arm. Peter grabs Greg's right arm as close to the wrist as possible with both hands and pushes it down to the ground, using his body weight to help pin Greg's right arm to the ground. This is a good time for Peter to apply a shoulder lock or knees to the head.

From the mount:

Peter is mounted on Greg, his eyes are always paying attention to the gun as he turns his shoulders to the left slightly. Greg pulls his pistol with his right hand. Peter turns to his own left and grabs Greg's right arm as close to the wrist as possible with both hands and pushes it down to the ground, using his body weight to help pin Greg's right arm to the ground. This is a good time for Peter to deliver an elbow.

From the closed guard:

Greg has Peter in his closed guard. This is one of the safest positions for Greg to transition or retain a weapon. Greg's pistol is on his right side. Greg wants to pull his pistol so he grabs and controls Peter's left wrist with his left hand, preventing Peter from using it to block Greg's reach for the pistol. As Peter tries to use his right hand to take away Greg's pistol, Greg simply turns to his right and lifts his left elbow up, using the forearm to block Peter's arm. Greg pulls the pistol and aims at Peter.

From the open guard:

Greg has Peter in his open guard, both feet pushing against Peter's hips to control the distance and both hands grabbing Peter's wrist and pulling his torso forward to keep him off balance. Greg changes the hand control as he uses his left hand to grab Peter's left wrist, pulling the arm across the body, while reaching for the pistol with his right hand. Greg pulls the pistol and aims it at Peter while still pulling the left arm with his left arm and pushing the feet against Peter's hips to keep him off balance.

FOLLOW UP TECHNIQUES

31, 35

TRANSITION LEVERAGE:
Weapon control and retention: X guard

The X-guard presents similar problems and solutions as other major positions when trying to control and retain your pistol. It is not as good for transitioning to the weapon as the guard but is sometimes easier to attain and can help neutralize the enemy's leverage. Greg demonstrates 3 options.

a

b

c

d

A Greg has Peter in his open guard but cannot place his feet and push Peter away as Peter is too close and bearing his weight forward. Greg uses the X-guard: he hooks the right foot inside Peter's left thigh and crosses the left leg in front of Peter with the shin blocking his hips and keeping the lower body distant. Greg's left hand grabs Peter's left shoulder with the forearm pressing against Peter's throat to keep the upper body distant. Greg reaches with his right hand for his pistol. Peter reaches for Greg's hand and pistol with his left hand. Greg turns the hand up in a counter-clockwise motion so the bottom of his hand points up, breaking Peter's grip. Greg pulls the pistol way back, raising it above his head, and points it at Peter. He then reaches and grabs Peter's left wrist with his left hand to prevent Peter from once again reaching to grab the pistol.

OPTIONAL TECHNIQUES

107

B Greg has X-guard on Peter's left leg, but this time Peter moved quickly and was able to grab Greg's right wrist and pin it to the ground with his left hand. Peter is using his body weight to keep Greg's wrist pinned so Greg cannot simply pull his hand out of the grip. Instead, Greg reaches with his left hand and grabs around the back of Peter's left elbow and pulls it forward, causing Peter's arm to buckle, while at the same time Greg extends his right arm, driving the pistol forward. Greg is able to free his hand and pistol with the same motion as in the previous technique. Greg continues to pull Peter's elbow and places the nose of the pistol on Peter's side.

C Greg has X-guard on Peter's right leg instead of the left as he turns to his right to reach for his pistol. Peter once again is able to pin Greg's arm to the ground. Greg uses the same motion to pull Peter's elbow forward, while at the same time, Greg extends his right arm, driving the pistol forward and regains control of his pistol.

X FOOT SWEEP

At times, when faced with the weapon on one side (in this case, Greg's right side) and the X-guard controlling his opposite leg (in this case, Peter's right leg), your opponent decides he can't get your weapon and may simply try to stand up and kick you or back away to get around your legs. In that case, this sweep is highly effective. At the end of the sweep, because he has the weapon, Greg prefers to stand up in base so he can reach for his pistol instead of going over the top for a side control or a mount position.

1 Greg has his pistol on his right side, is turned to his right and uses the X-guard to control Peter's right leg, Greg's left foot hooks Peter's right thigh and the right shin is in front of Peter's hips to block them. Peter plants his hands on Greg's stomach and pushes off it to stand up and get away. Peter steps forward with his left foot and Greg immediately grabs the back of the heel with his right hand. As Peter stands up, Greg keeps his left foot hooked on Peter's right thigh and places his right foot on his left hip. He grabs Peter's left wrist with his left hand, pulling it across his body.

REVERSE

1 Notice Greg's left foot hooks right behind Peter's right knee.

a

b

2 Greg extends his right leg, pushing Peter's hips back while at the same time he kicks his left foot up, forcing Peter's right leg forward. Since Greg also controls his left foot, Peter cannot step back and regain his base and falls to the ground. Greg uses Peter's momentum to help himself up by holding on to the arm and the heel. As Peter's back hits the ground Greg plants his right hand back of his body and stands up in base (technique #1) and is ready to draw his weapon.

c

a

b

3 Alternatively, as Greg stands up, Peter may attempt to stand up as well, so Greg reaches with his left hand and grabs Peter's left pant leg at the cuff and pulls it up to keep Peter on the ground. Greg steps forward with his left leg as he pulls Peter's leg to his left and drives his left knee just past Peter's thigh. Greg pivots off his feet so he can face Peter as he draws his pistol.

c

OPTIONAL TECHNIQUES

1

TAKEDOWN FROM THE FRONT

You may be on patrol – standing, walking, running or engaging the enemy – and you may be surprised by the enemy and tackled from the front. Since Greg has his right hand controlling the butt of the rifle, Peter comes from the front right.

1 Greg may be engaging the enemy when Peter surprises him and tackles him from the front right, taking him down.

2 Greg immediately wants to separate himself from Peter so he can use his weapons, so he places his left foot on Peter's right hip and the right hand on his left shoulder and pushes himself away. Greg grabs Peter's left arm with his right hand and pulls him forward until he is off balance and falling forward. Greg switches hands and grabs Peter's arm with his left hand, pulling it across his body so he can use his right hand to draw his pistol. Notice how Greg coils his right arm back so the pistol is far away from Peter's reach.

TAKEDOWN FROM THE SIDES

In this case, Peter surprises and tackles Greg from his blind side. Greg has his right hand controlling the butt of the rifle, so Peter comes from the front left.

1 Greg is on patrol and Peter surprises and tackles him from the blind side.

2 As Peter tackles both his legs for a takedown, Greg wants to fall to the side of the weapon and prevent Peter from getting it. Greg immediately hooks his back foot (here, his left foot) on Peter's right leg and pivots off his right foot to protect his weapon from Peter's reach. Greg uses his left arm posted on Peter's head and uses his right foot on Peter's left hip to keep distance and retain control over his rifle and pistol.

REVERSE

2 Notice Greg's left hand pushes the right side of Peter's head and his right foot pushes Peter's left hip to drive him away and to the right.

3 Greg releases Peter's head and grabs Peter's left arm with his left hand to pull him across his body while pushing the hips with both feet until he is off balance and falling forward. Greg pulls Peter's arm across his body so he can use his right hand to draw his pistol.

TAKEDOWN FROM THE BACK

In this case, Greg is attacked from behind. Again, Greg's main concern is to protect his weapons and fall to the side where his pistol is and have the nose of his rifle point up. Greg's right hand controls the butt of the rifle and the pistol is on his right side.

a

1 Greg is tackled from behind. As he starts to go down he turns his torso to his left so as to fall on his right side and have the nose of his rifle point up. Greg plants his right hand on the ground to control his fall and steps forward with his right leg.

b

c

2 Greg drops forward on his right knee and arm and as he falls to his right, kicks his left leg back and to his right, hooking his foot on the outside of Peter's right hip. As Greg continues to fall to his right, his left shin is in front of Peter's hips keeping distance. Greg uses his left hand to push Peter's head to the left, puts his right foot on Peter's left hip and pushes off it, keeping Peter away.

REVERSE

2 Check out how Greg falls to his right side, keeping the pistol and the rifle away from Peter. Also, notice how he hooks his left foot on the outside of Peter's hip. His knee points in to his right so as he falls to the ground he can bring it up, locking his shin in front of Peter's hips.

3 Having created the proper distance, Greg switches his left hand from Peter's head and grabs the left wrist instead, pulling the arm across his body as he turns to his left so he can center his body and face Peter. Greg draws his pistol with the right hand, aiming it to the head.

OUTSIDE TRIP WITH THE M4 RIFLE

The same outside trip works very well when clinching the enemy while in possession of your weapon. In this case, Peter uses both hands to block and try to gain control of the weapon. Greg uses the outside trip to take Peter down and retain his weapon.

1 Greg clinches Peter, keeping the rifle in front of Peter and the barrel pointing to the right. Peter grabs the rifle with both hands as he tries to block and take it away. Greg hooks his left leg around the back of Peter's right leg as he drops his body down so his head presses against Peter's stomach. Greg keeps the rifle pointing away from Peter.

2 Greg does the outside trip as before but his right hand remains in control of the weapon and makes sure the barrel doesn't hit the ground head on. Once Peter lands on his back, Greg reaches for his pistol with his right hand. He then extends his right leg out, puts his left hand on the Peter's face and pushes off it to raise his body, pointing the gun at Peter's chest.

H2H TECHNIQUE 112

HAND GUN: *Two hands*

Note: If you are going to take the time to train on firearm takeaways, you must learn how to use them and understand the difference between various firearms. There are two common types of handguns; one is a semi-automatic, it has a slide that moves forward and back. If you are holding the barrel when it goes off, you may damage your hand, but most likely it will become jammed. It is important that, if you get control of the handgun, you know how to clear the jammed round so you can fire the weapon. The revolver is not as common. It has a cylinder that spins if you can hold the cylinder from spinning the weapon will not fire. Guns are very loud. Even if you know it is going to go off, you will still be startled and you ears will ring.

In this scenario, your adversary has a gun and is holding it with two hands while standing in front of you. This method will work even if your adversary is holding it with one hand. Here is one method to counter this situation.

1 Aitor has his gun out and is pointing it at Greg. Greg slowly raises his hand in a non-threatening manner, then pushes off his right foot and pivots off the left one, turning his torso to the right and away from the path of the shot. At the same time Greg grabs the back of the gun and the top of Aitor's hand with his left hand, using a stiff arm to prevent Aitor from pointing the gun back at him.

2 Without losing control over the gun, Greg steps forward with his left foot and grabs the barrel of the gun with the right hand, as he pushes it down and away from him he puts his head and shoulder under Aitor's in order to keep control in case of a struggle (also, if Aitor pulls away, Greg can pin him against the wall or another object). Notice that Greg grabs under the barrel of the gun with the right palm facing up so he has the most control of the weapon.

OPTIONAL TECHNIQUES

111

3 Greg twists the gun in a counter-clockwise direction until the barrel points straight back toward Aitor. He then pulls the barrel back, forcing it against Aitor's thumb and pulling it out of Aitor's hands.

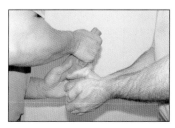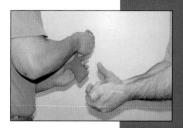

HAND GUN: *One hand*

This time, Greg's opponent holds the gun with one hand only. Greg uses the same evasive action to escape the shot but adjusts the controlling grip because a single hand controls the gun.

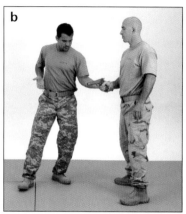
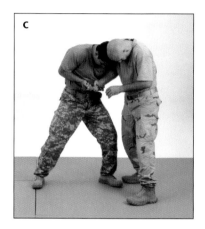

1 Aitor has his gun out and is pointing it at Greg, using one hand to grip the gun. Greg pushes off his right foot and pivots off the left, turning his torso to the right and away from the path of the shot. At the same time, Greg grabs the under the back of Aitor's wrist with his left hand, using a stiff arm to prevent Aitor from pointing the gun back at him. Greg steps forward with the left leg as he reaches and grabs under the barrel with the right hand. Greg has to control the gun and prevent Aitor from simply passing it to the free hand.

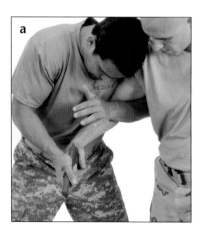
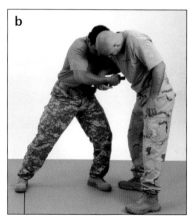
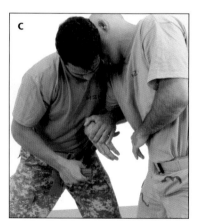

2 Greg slides the left arm back to hook it behind Aitor's elbow, stopping him from pulling or stripping the arm and the gun back. Greg drives the barrel back towards Aitor's body with the right hand. From there, Greg applies the wrist lock, using his left hand to pull in Aitor's right hand.

3 Keeping the wrist lock on Aitor, Greg pulls the right arm back as he swings his own right arm back and brings it forward, delivering a blow to Aitor's face with the barrel of the gun.

 If Greg doesn't keep his head and chest close to Aitor, Aitor can use his other hand to block Greg's control and strip the gun away.

a

b

c

HAND GUN VICTIM

In this case, Aitor is pointing the gun at Greg's partner. Aitor holds the gun with both hands.

1 Aitor points his gun at Peter. Greg sneaks from the side and grabs Aitor's gun in the same fashion as in the two-hand technique described in technique #113. Greg's left hand grabs the back of the gun over Aitor's thumb and the right hand grabs under the barrel. Greg pushes the gun down and away from Peter so if a shot is fired it will miss both Peter and himself.

OPTIONAL TECHNIQUES

111

RIFLE

In this situation, Aitor leads Greg with his rifle pressing against Greg's back. Greg needs to look for the proper moment to act, he may wait for a possible distraction before he turns or simply go right away and surprise the enemy.

1 Aitor presses his rifle against Greg's back. Greg looks over his right shoulder to check Aitor's stance and notes which leg is back. In this case Aitor has his right leg back so his torso is open to the right. Greg pivots to his right and hooks his right arm under and around Aitor's rifle. Greg grabs the top of the rifle with his right hand and pulls it down while he controls the barrel of the rifle. His right shoulder and biceps lock the weapon in place.

2 Greg pivots off his right foot and grabs the back of Aitor's head with the left hand. It is very important that Greg keeps the rifle sandwiched between him and Aitor so that Aitor can't just pull away and line the rifle up for a shot. He then delivers a knee strike to the groin and a head butt, or both. (If you can, pin him against a wall or object.)

a b c

3 Greg grabs the rifle strap with his left hand and pulls it over Aitor's head (if there is a strap on the gun). Greg holds the barrel higher than Aitor's left hand and over his right, then violently forces Aitor's right hand down and over his left, striking the left side of Aitor's face with the barrel in the process. Immediately adjust for adversary to try and recover.

OPTIONAL TECHNIQUES

111

ANATOMY OF TECHNIQUES

J) Torso

KNIFE: *Offense*

Stance

Weapon on weapon:

When faced with an enemy who also wields a weapon, Greg
will use this stance.

1 Greg holds his knife with the right hand. He has his right foot forward, the left one back. His
knife points slightly inwards with the blade pointing down and out. Greg has his elbows close
to his body and uses his arms to protect his side while the forearms protect from frontal strikes.
Greg's left hand is in front of his chest ready to parry any direct strikes. Notice how Greg compacts
his body: his shoulders are drawn in and forward and the head is down, giving the opponent a min-
imal target on his vital areas.

Weapon on unarmed adversary:

When the enemy has no weapon, Greg uses this stance.

1 Greg switches the position of his feet. His right hand holds the knife, and he has his right foot back. The left arm is forward to block any attempts from his enemy to take away the knife. Greg holds his knife back, making it difficult for his enemy to grab it and allowing Greg a greater range of strike choices.

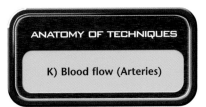

ANATOMY OF TECHNIQUES

K) Blood flow (Arteries)

KNIFE ON KNIFE DEFENSE

Don't ever underestimate the danger of facing an enemy with a knife, especially if he is skilled in the use of the weapon, he can inflict tremendous wounds or even kill you quickly. Escape so you have time to transition to your weapon, pick something up or run!

Note: It is always important to attack the weapon hand first and then move to the vital areas.

Inside

Greg demonstrates several defenses to a knife attack. In the first case, Aitor attacks Greg with an inside stab.

1 When Aitor strikes, Greg arches his body, bringing his hips back so his vital organs are far from the strike. Greg blocks Aitor's knife hand with his left hand, steps back and cuts the top of Aitor's wrist with his own knife.

2 Greg pushes Aitor's knife hand away with his left hand and coils his own right arm back so he can stab Aitor's chest or neck.

Outside

This time Aitor takes a swipe with the knife coming from the outside

1 When Aitor strikes, Greg arches his body, bringing his hips back so his vital organs are far from the strike. Greg uses his left hand to block Aitor's right hand motion. He holds the outside of the hand and cuts the wrist with his knife. Greg uses his hold on Aitor's right hand to pull the right arm across his body as he steps outside, much like in an arm-drag, and slashes Aitor's throat. Notice Greg's position of the arm that controls the knife. His movements are compact, the arm bent at the elbow and the hand always bent at 90° in relation to the forearm with the cutting part of the blade facing the enemy.

Escape low line:

Aitor attacks with the knife in a low line. Greg arches his body back and swings the left arm down, using his forearm bent at the elbow and parallel to the ground to block Aitor's forearm while at the same time Greg uses his right palm to strike Aitor's face. Having successfully defended the initial stab, Greg immediately turns and runs away so he can either transition to a secondary weapon or grab an object to use against the knife.

Escape high line:

Aitor delivers a high line knife attack. Greg steps forward and to the right and swings the left forearm out, using his forearm bent at the elbow and parallel to the ground to block Aitor's forearm while at the same time Greg uses his right palm to strike Aitor's face. Having successfully defended the initial stab, Greg immediately turns and runs away so he can either transition to a secondary weapon or grab an object to use against the knife.

ANATOMY OF TECHNIQUES

K) Blood flow (Arteries)

Takeaway

When the attacker goes for an upwards stab, this is a great technique both to defend the strike and to take his knife away.

1 Aitor takes an upward stab with his knife. Greg always worries about getting cut so he arches his back, moving his hips and vital organs away. He places his left forearm at the elbow and right hand at Aitor's wrist to block the attack. Greg then wraps his left arm around Aitor's right arm above the elbow while keeping his head in tight against Aitor's shoulder for better control and to take away space for Aitor to counter.

2 Greg pulls Aitor's right arm out with his hand on the wrist and slightly turns it to that the elbow is facing up and drives his left shoulder and chest down against Aitor's shoulder and elbow, forcing him to bend down or have his elbow snap. Greg slides his hand down the arm to Aitor's hand and applies a wrist lock, pushing the hand in against the forearm. Greg continues to pull up on Aitor's arm, forcing him to the ground.

REVERSE

2 Notice how Greg controls Aitor's arm with his left arm wrapped around Aitor's above the elbow. Greg's shoulder presses down on Aitor's shoulder and his right hand applies a wristlock.

Continuing with the reverse angle: Alternatively, Greg may simply drive Aitor's knife to the ground with a solid strike or push, causing it to slide up and out of Aitor's grip so Greg can simply pull it away.

DETAIL

Takeaway: Counter-grabbing at the knife

It is very important for Greg to keep his head pressed against Aitor's chest/shoulder. Otherwise Aitor can slip his left arm in front and pull the knife away, as in the handgun example demonstrated in technique #113, or pass the knife to the other hand.

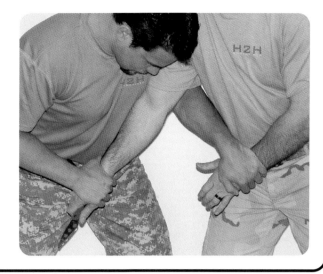

Knife on stick

When facing an enemy with a knife, always try to find an object such as a stick, a baton or a rock, and use it to defend against the knife. When striking or countering, always attack the hand with the knife.

1 Aitor has the knife in his right hand and pulls it back as he readies to strike. Greg has a stick in his right hand and is in fighting stance with his weight on the front leg and the stick out, ready to counter-strike. When Aitor strikes, Greg pushes off his right foot and pivots his body back and to the left, moving his vital organs back away from the knife. At the same time Greg swings his right arm in, striking Aitor's hand with the stick. The impact of the stick against the hand generally causes the attacker to drop the knife.

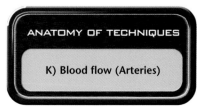

ANATOMY OF TECHNIQUES

K) Blood flow (Arteries)

HAND TO HAND
H2H®
COMBAT

STRIKING

To be a complete fighter, in addition to mastering grappling techniques, one needs to know how to strike. While H2H combat mostly revolves around grappling, there are moments even in a grappling situation when striking is effective and even necessary. In this section you learn the basic fundamentals of striking, including punching, kicking and blocking. Additionally, you will learn how to use pads as targets for striking.

STANCES

Being able to maintain a proper stance is extremely important in a fight. When you have the proper stance you have the optimal position to both defend and deliver strikes.

Ready:
Greg is trying to diffuse a situation. It is very dangerous for him to stand within striking distance of a potential threat with his hand down. Action is faster than reaction. Greg takes this non-threatening stance, which is almost a fighting stance, so he can react. Before a fight begins, Greg is ready for anything. This is not a threatening stance but a ready stance. Greg has his left leg forward with the foot pointing forward. His right leg is back with the foot pointing at 45°. His body is at a 45° angle to his opponent. His elbows are close to his body, the forearms are up slightly, and the hands are open in a non-threatening manner but ready to strike or block any strikes. The head is slightly tucked in with the chin close to the chest to give a small target to the opponent.

Fighting stance:
When the fight begins, you want to be in this stance. It is similar to the ready stance but Greg's knees are more deeply bent, giving him explosive spring off his legs to deliver kicks and to move away. Greg's forearms are tucked closer to his chest with the hands closed in fists and the shoulders hunched forward. The hands are in front of his face protecting his chin. Footwork: always step first with the foot closest to the direction of the movement, i.e. if Greg were stepping forward, he would first step with his left leg, set the foot down and then step forward with the right.

OPEN HAND STRIKES

Palm strike

Palm strikes are good to use so you do not break your hand.
It is hard to transition to a weapon with a broken hand.

Base palm:

Greg shoots his arm forward in a jabbing motion, striking Aitor's face with the base of his palm. Notice how Greg's fingers are pulled back so that the hand sticks to the face, or raises the chin for a strike or knock off balance.

All of the hand:

Greg uses the same motion as before but this time the entire hand is involved in the strike. Greg does not pull the fingers back.

Eye gouge

Thumb:

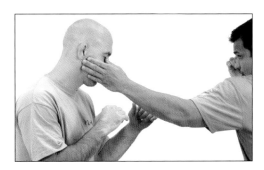

Greg shoots the arm forward with the hand perpendicular to the ground and his thumb is slightly out from the hand. Greg uses Aitor's face to help guide the thumb into the eye.

Tip of the fingers:

Similar to the previous strike, but here Greg's hand is parallel to the ground with the palm facing down and the fingers spread so as to strike Aitor's eye.

PUNCHES

Provided you do not break your hand, punching is one of the fastest ways to knockout your assailant. It is also good to disorient your assailant so that you can move to another position.

1-6 Punch

1 Jab: Pushing off his right leg, Greg extends his left arm to deliver a straight jab to Aitor's chin. The jab is a straight-line punch with the fist shooting straight from its ready place to the target (usually the chin). The fist moves in a corkscrew motion as it starts perpendicular to the ground and turns in a clockwise direction until the fist is parallel to the ground as it strikes the target. Greg keeps his right arm close to his body.

2 Right cross: Pushing off his right foot, Greg shoots his right hip forward as he launches his right hand in a parabolic trajectory. The cross is a looping punch that is launched from the back hand towards the enemy's face.

3 Left hook: As he coils his right arm back from the right cross, Greg pushes off his left foot. He pivots off the toes of his feet and turns his hips to the right as he launches the left hook. The hook has a more circular trajectory than the cross. Greg uses the power generated by the momentum of his hips to add power to all his punches. The hook generally targets the chin or the body.

4 Overhand right: Greg continues his sequence with an overhand right as he pulls the left hook back, pivots off his toes again and turns his hips to the left as he loops the right hand over Aitor's hands. The overhand right has a similar trajectory as the cross; a parabola slightly flatter than the hook.

5 Left uppercut: Greg dips his body slightly, flexing the knees, and pushes off his left foot as he shoots the left uppercut. The uppercut trajectory is a shorter, more compact one. The fist starts low and shoots up, generally targeting the chin.

6 Right uppercut: Greg uses the same motion as the left uppercut – he dips his body, twists the hips to the left and pushes off the right foot, driving his body up as his fist shoots up to strike the chin. The uppercut is a great punch to break the opponent's defense and strike the face.

REVERSE

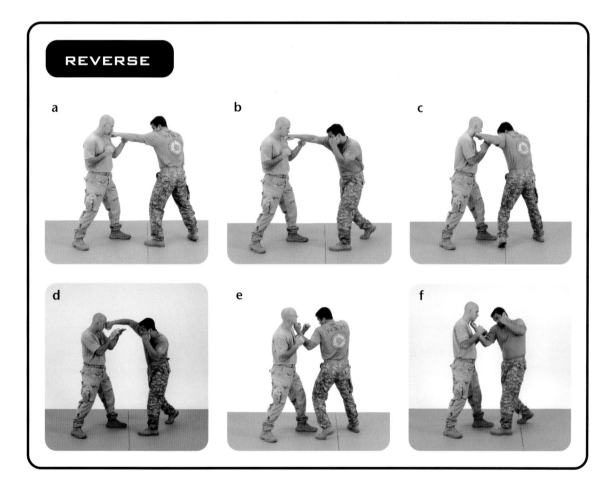

a

b

c

d

e

f

ANATOMY OF TECHNIQUES

C) Brain Stem D) Skull
E) Boxers Fracture
J) Torso B) Nerves in neck

BRACHIAL STUN KNIFE HAND

The knife hand works best for striking the neck. It can slip under the chin and over the shoulder to penetrate through the muscles to the nerves in the side of the neck, causing a knockout. Or, if you hit in the windpipe in the front of the throat, it can cause serious injury, or even death.

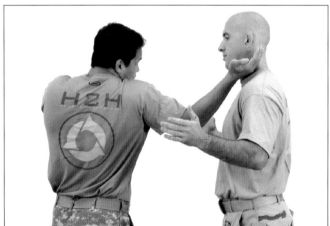

1 Greg slides his right hand over his head as if he were combing his hair and explosively pushes off his right foot. He pivots off his toes and turns his hips to the left as he chops down with the open hand, striking Aitor's neck with the bottom edge of the palm of his right hand. Notice Greg's hand position: all fingers together pointing forward and the thumb closed in forming a knife.

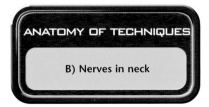

ANATOMY OF TECHNIQUES

B) Nerves in neck

HEAD BUTTS

Front

Greg grabs Aitor's hands. He pulls Aitor's hands, as his hips move slightly forward, pushes off with his back foot and drives his head down and forward, striking Aitor's chin or nose. Notice Greg strikes the target with the top of his forehead. This works just as well without the hand. If someone is in your face, it is a great way to start your assault because it is hard to defend.

Thai Clinch

From the Thai clinch, Greg pulls Aitor's head towards him as he pushes off his back foot and drives his head down and forward, striking Aitor's chin

Rear

When Greg is clinched from the rear, he bends his knees, drops down and then pushes off his feet, exploding upwards as he shoots his head back and strikes Aitor's face.

ANATOMY OF TECHNIQUES

C) Brain Stem D) Skull

Greg demonstrates various elbow strikes.

Elbows in:

Greg is in a fighting stance. As the opponent comes in to clinch, Greg pushes off his right foot, twists his torso and hips to the left and brings the right elbow across, striking the opponent's face. Note that the left forearm is tucked in so that if the opponent tries to clinch, Greg can defend. Greg then pushes off the left foot and repeats the motion to the opposite side, delivering a left elbow strike.

Elbows down:

Greg pushes off his right foot and shoots the right elbow up in a circular motion, coming down and striking the opponent's head. Note that the left forearm is tucked in so if the opponent tries to clinch, Greg can defend. Greg repeats the motion to the opposite side, pushing off his left foot and delivering a downward left elbow strike.

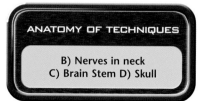

ANATOMY OF TECHNIQUES

B) Nerves in neck
C) Brain Stem D) Skull

Elbows up:

Using a similar push/pivoting combination, Greg shoots his elbows up this time.

a

b

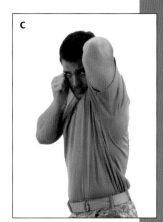
c

EXAMPLES

The dynamics of the elbow strikes. Notice how Greg pivots his shoulders and hips to add power to the strikes.

a

b

c

Rear strikes:

When clinched from the rear, Greg uses a rear elbow. He holds Aitor's right wrist with his left hand to prevent Aitor from spinning or grabbing his weapon. Greg turns his shoulders to the right as he delivers a right elbow to Aitor's face.

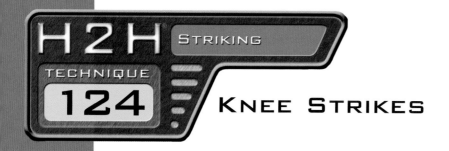

KNEE STRIKES

Thai clinch stomach

1 Greg has Aitor in a Thai clinch and has his right leg back. He pulls Aitor's head towards him and, pushing off the right foot, drives the right knee forward into Aitor's stomach.

a 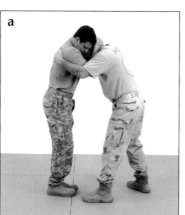 **b** 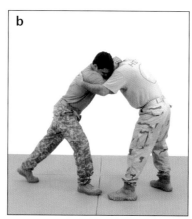 **c**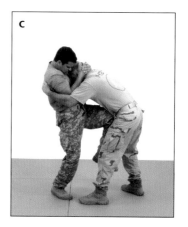

2 Greg drops the right foot back to the ground, takes a big step back with his left leg and shoots the knee forward as he pulls Aitor's head towards him, striking him in the stomach.

Head

Greg pulls Aitor's head down as he shoots the right knee up and strikes Aitor's face. Notice, to hit the head, Greg shoots the knee up and not forward as in the previous stomach strike.

Thigh

 When Aitor is sideways, Greg delivers a knee strike to the side of the thigh. If Greg is facing him and Aitor leans back with his hips, Greg strikes the front of the thigh.

Groin

When he has Aitor clinched around the waist and is close in, Greg doesn't have enough space to effectively deliver knee strikes to the stomach or head so he opts for the groin strike. Greg pulls Aitor forward as he shoots his knee forward and up, striking the groin.

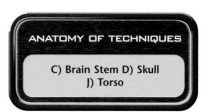

ANATOMY OF TECHNIQUES

C) Brain Stem D) Skull
J) Torso

Snap kick

The snap kick is a short and sharp motion. From a fighting stance, Greg lifts his knee up and snaps the foot out, striking the target with the ball or top of the foot. This is a very quick kick, particularly when targeting the groin.

Front kick: rear leg

With his rear leg, Greg pushes off the right foot, lifts the knee up and thrusts the foot forward, striking the target with the bottom of the foot. This is not a snap motion but rather a thrusting motion, which makes this a slower but more powerful kick than the snap kick. Greg leads with the heel of the foot during the striking motion.

Front kick: front leg

For a front leg front kick, Greg pushes off his front leg and raises the knee up, putting his weight mostly on the back leg. He then pushes off the back leg and extends the front leg, thrusting the foot forward and striking Aitor. Again, this is a power kick, and is good at creating space for a weapon transition.

Leg kick

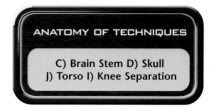

ANATOMY OF TECHNIQUES

C) Brain Stem D) Skull
J) Torso I) Knee Separation

1 Pushing off his right foot, Greg swings the right leg around, hitting the outside of Aitor's left thigh.

a

b

c

2 He then drops the right foot back to the fighting stance and switches to the inside strike. Greg throws a left palm strike to Aitor's face as he pivots his right foot out. Greg shoots the left leg forward, striking the inside of Aitor's left thigh.

Oblique kick

Greg pushes off his right foot and steps forward, striking Aitor's knee with the bottom of his right foot. Note that Greg's toes are pointing out. This works well with a clinch.

Round kick

1 right - Greg turns the left foot out so his toes point to the left and turns his hips to the left. Greg pushes off his right foot as he brings the right knee up and then kicks his right leg at waist level, striking Aitor's mid-section with the top of his foot.

a

b

a

b

c

2 switch – Greg returns the right foot to the start position, then steps out to the right with it toes pointing out turning his hips to the right. Greg pushes off his left foot, lifts the knee up and kicks the left leg out, striking Aitor's mid-section with the top of his shin. Caution: Kicking this way without hard shoes can cause fractures in small bones of the foot, particularly if it hits the opponent's elbow.

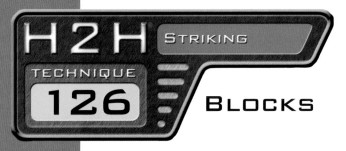

BLOCKS

Being able to effectively block strikes during an assault can be the difference between survival and death. Greg demonstrates the most common and effective blocks for fighting.

Parrys:

Left Jab: When Aitor throws a left jab, Greg pushes off his right leg and turns his hips and shoulders to the left, using the top of the right forearm or lower palm to deflect the punch.

Right Cross: Aitor throws a right cross. Greg pushes off his left foot and turns his hips and shoulder to the right, using the top of the left forearm to strike and deflect the punch.

Rhino

Right: Greg has his fists close and in front, protecting his face. When a right punch comes, Greg turns his shoulders to the right, grabs the back of his head with the left hand and moves the elbow in front of the face, blocking the punch with the arm.

Left: When a left punch comes, Greg turns his shoulders to the left, grabs the back of his own head with the right hand and moves the elbow in front of the face, blocking the punch with the arm. Notice how compact Greg is with his elbows, fists and arms protecting his head.

Slip

Aitor throws a left-right punch combination, flexing the right leg and Greg dips his shoulders and head to the right just enough to avoid the left jab. As Aitor delivers the right cross, Greg flexes both legs and dips his head under the punch as he pushes off the right foot and swings his head to the left.

Leg Check

Shin to shin: Greg lifts the left knee up and points it out to the left with the leg straight down and the toes pointing down, checking Aitor's right kick and blocking Aitor's shin with his shin. This occurs when Aitor and Greg are close together.

Shin to Foot: Greg is able to intercept the kick in the same manner, but this time, when Aitor kicks, Greg angles the top of his shin to intercept Aitor's foot. This can cause damage to Aitor's foot. Shin on shin is just pain, but if the foot meets the shin, then it may break.

Block

Round Kick: Aitor throws a roundhouse right kick. Greg pushes off the right foot, pivots to the left and blocks the kick with his arms. Note Greg's arm's position; the left elbow is tight against his side, the forearm is up with the fist protecting his face. Greg's right arm is bent with the elbow at his side and the forearm parallel to the ground, protecting the bottom kicks.

Catch: After blocking the kick, Greg grabs Aitor's leg by wrapping his left arm around the calf. Greg now can either strike back or trip Aitor.

Feint

Greg pushes off his toes and pulls his hips back to avoid a kick, knife or stick strike. This is an easy way to avoid the counter.

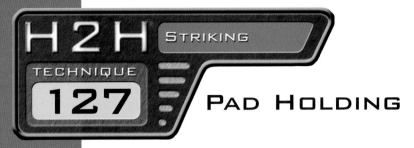

PAD HOLDING

Many people get injured because they hold the striking pads improperly. Often times, they not only injure themselves, but their training partner as well. Greg and Aitor demonstrate the proper way to hold the pads for various striking situations.

Note: You should cross punch the pads so you will not hit your holder. It is also good for developing hip movement. When holding, try to meet your partner's strike against the pad with a little force to protect your shoulder and abdomen from abuse.

Thai Pads Punches

Jab and Cross: While the pads are up for the jab, shoot the pad forward to meet the cross.

Hook: Bring the pad in front, almost perpendicular to the striker, giving him a target for the hook.

Over hand: Pad is lower with the top pointing back.

Uppercut: Pad faces down and in the center.

Mitt Punches

A similar technique and position is used when working with the mitt to practice punches. Use the mitt to meet the strikers punches, giving him a target and enough pressure for him to feel his power.

Thai Pads Elbows

Circular: Pads are perpendicular to the ground.

Uppercut: Pads are at a 45° angle to the ground and facing down.

Down: Pads are at a 45°angle to the ground and facing up.

Head Butts

Place the front pad parallel to the ground with this elbow points out. The back pad is perpendicular to the ground with the elbow pointing down with the hand backing the front pad.

Knees

Pads are butted against each other with the top pad facing forward and the bottom pad facing down.

Kicks

Round: Pads face out and are perpendicular to the ground, butted up against each other.

Front: Pads are butted against each other with the top pad facing forward and the bottom pad facing down.

Pad Holder Throws mitts to develop reflexes and feints

1 Aitor throws a wild right. Greg uses the rhino block to defend, then on the second one, Greg dips and slips under the punch.

2 Aitor follows with a wild left and Greg dips under again.

3 Aitor throws a straight right and Greg uses the rhino block to defend.

Training Equipment

WRAPPING THE HANDS

Although you may think that punching someone will cause damage to them, it may also cause you to break your hand (see (E) Boxers Fracture). Properly striking is always the key. However, if you are going to be in a professional or amateur fight you need to know how to use your hands. Wrapping the hands is one of the most important things a fighter can do before a fight. By properly wrapping the hands, you protect your knuckles and bones of the hand from breaking.

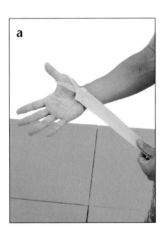

1 Start out with an open palm. Hook the loop around your thumb while pulling the tape with the opposite hand. Maintain a slight tension on the tape but not too much otherwise at the end of the wrap you will have cut the circulation to your fingers. Pull the tape down over the palm of your hand and loop it under the junction of the wrist, then pull it up and around the wrist. Continue wrapping the tape around the palm in the same direction. This time, wrap it around the middle of the back of the hand. Now the tape is coming down in front of the wrist.

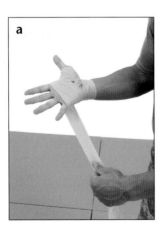

2 Pull the tape down and back and wrap it under the wrist again. This time, however, instead of looping around the wrist, pull it up and in front of the thumb, then pull it down behind the hand. Pull the tape up in front of the hand and go around the back of the thumb yet again.

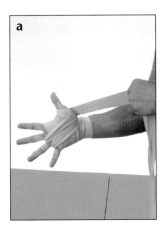

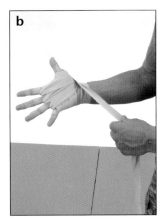

3 Pull the tape and wrap around each finger. At every loop make sure to come back around the thumb until all the fingers have been wrapped once. Then go back around the thumb, down the back of the wrist, up the back of the hand and loop around the hand to secure the finger loops in place.

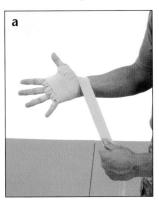

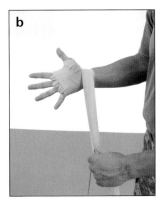

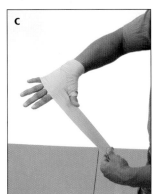

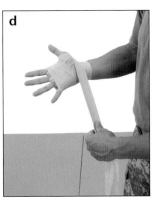

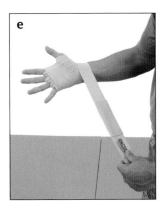

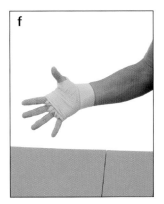

4 Do two more complete loops around the hand. On the second one, pull the tape back around the loop once again around the wrist. Continue wrapping the tape around the hand and the wrist until you run out of tape.

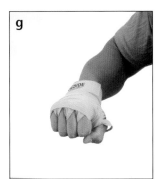

ANATOMY OF TECHNIQUES

E) Boxers Fracture

A) *Pressure Point:* Some people try to use pressure points as the solution to many problems. They are best used when you are in a control position over an opponent, or you just want to encourage him or her to move or give up something.

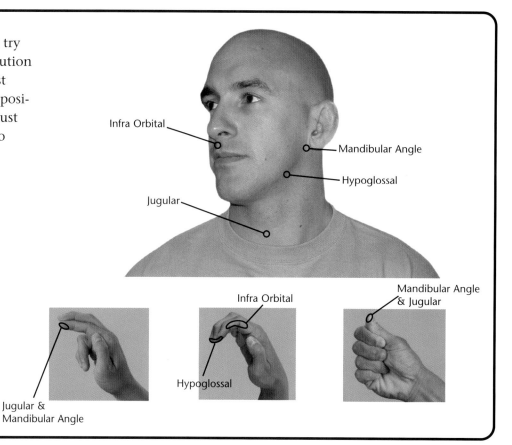

B) *The neck:* A strike to the nerves on side of the neck can result in loss of motor skills or a knockout. A strike to the front of the neck can cause the larynx or windpipe to temporally collapse or it could stay collapsed causing death.

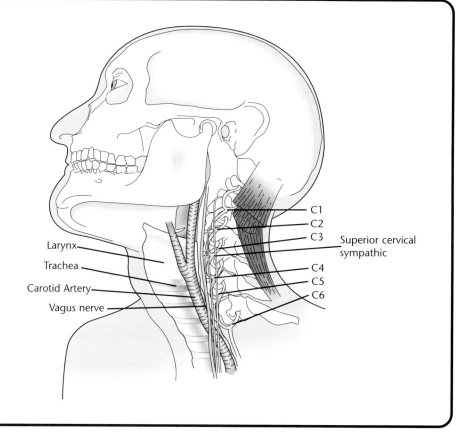

C) _Brain Stem_ – The knockout: There are two common ways to get knocked out from a strike to the head. When the head gets struck hard, the brain can get knocked against the inside of skull causing a knockout. This can cause a headache, concussion, the brain to swell or even death. The other way to get knocked out happens most of the time from strikes to the lower part of the skull or jaw. There are nerves that run up through the base of the skull to the brain that send information to parts of the body like the legs. It is very common in fighting events to see someone take a hard shot to the jaw and their knees get wobbly and they lose all motor skills. If you get hit with your chin up it does not take much to get knocked out. But, if your chin is down and shoulders up, you can take a much harder shot.

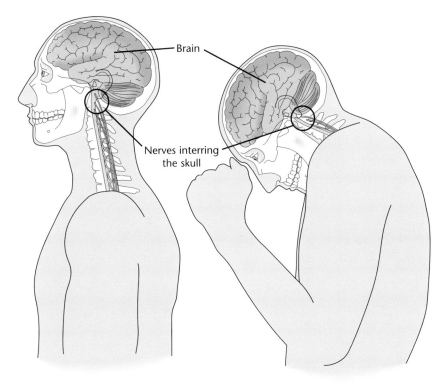

Brain

Nerves interring
the skull

D) _Skull_ – Common fractures to the face shown here.

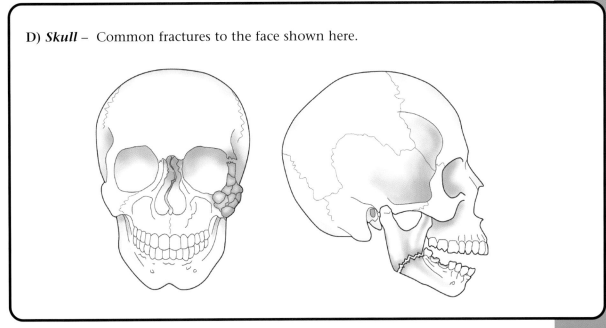

E) *Boxers Fracture* – A common fracture that occurs as a result of a punch is the boxer's fracture, as shown here. Since it will be hard to use your weapon if you break your hand punching the enemy, using palm or elbow strikes may be better striking options. This way you won't risk breaking your hand.

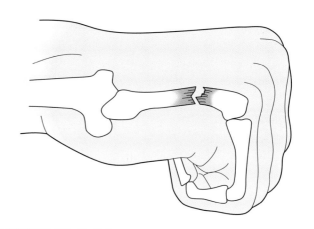

F) *Kimura Separation* – This picture illustrates the parts of the shoulder joint that are damaged as a result of a submission hold such as a Kimura.

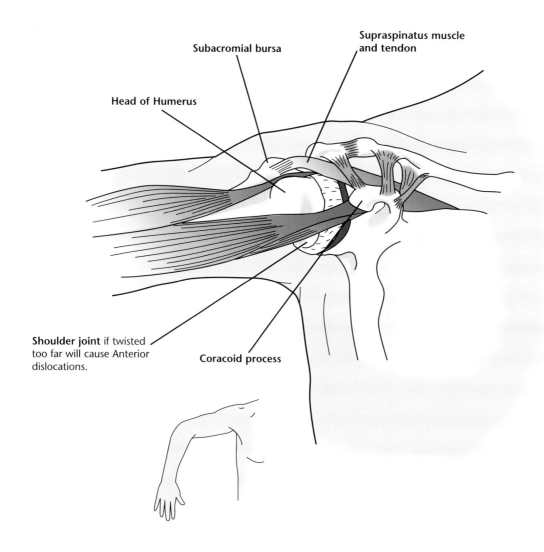

Subacromial bursa

Supraspinatus muscle and tendon

Head of Humerus

Shoulder joint if twisted too far will cause Anterior dislocations.

Coracoid process

G) *Bent Arm Bar Separation* – This picture illustrates the parts of the shoulder joint that are damaged as a result of a submission hold, such as a Bent Arm Bar.

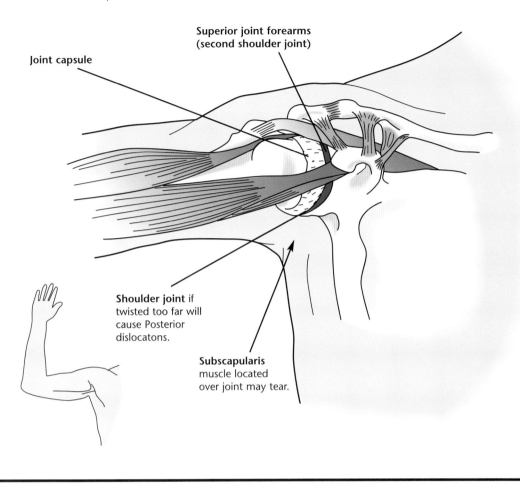

Joint capsule

Superior joint forearms
(second shoulder joint)

Shoulder joint if twisted too far will cause Posterior dislocatons.

Subscapularis muscle located over joint may tear.

H) *Elbow Separation* – A common occurrence from an arm-lock is shown here with an elbow hyper-extension causing a dislocation or ligament tear and capsule fracture.

Biceps tendon

Radial annular ligament

Joint capsule

Radius bone

Ulna bone

Ulnar collateral ligaments

Humerus bone

I) *Knee Separation* – A properly applied side-kick to the knee joint may cause ligament tear to the knee.

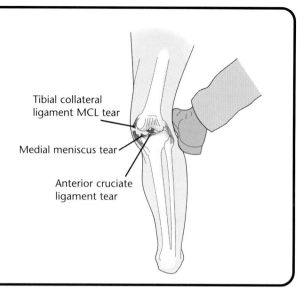

Tibial collateral ligament MCL tear

Medial meniscus tear

Anterior cruciate ligament tear

J) *Torso* — The vital areas of the Torso region.

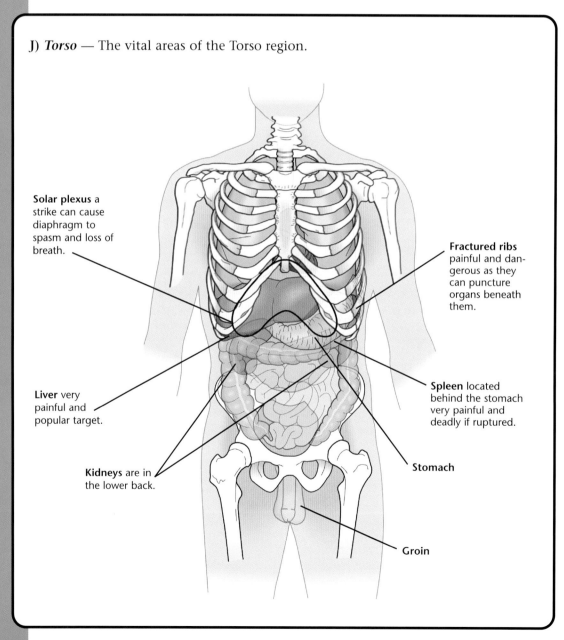

Solar plexus a strike can cause diaphragm to spasm and loss of breath.

Fractured ribs painful and dangerous as they can puncture organs beneath them.

Liver very painful and popular target.

Spleen located behind the stomach very painful and deadly if ruptured.

Kidneys are in the lower back.

Stomach

Groin

K) *Blood flow (Arteries)*: The choke, if applied properly, will shut the arteries on both sides of the neck, causing unconsciousness or if held too long death.

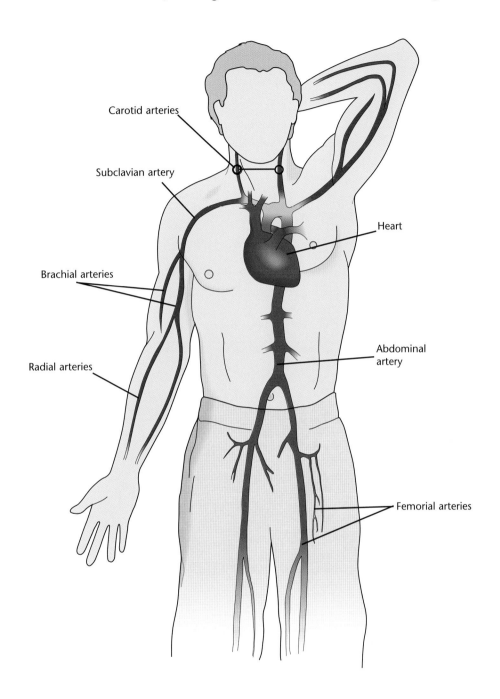

Knife cuts & stabs chart	Chart can vary due to size and heart rate		
Name	Depth below surface	Loss of consciousness	Death
Cartotid artery	1½"	5 sec.	12 sec.
Subclavian	2½"	2 sec.	3½ sec.
Heart	3½"	1 sec.	3 sec.
Brachial	½"	14 sec.	90 sec.
Abdominal	5"	1 sec	
Radial	¼"	30 sec.	120 sec.
Femoral artery	2"	25 sec.	80 sec.

CROSSFIT FITNESS PROGRAM:

CrossFit is a strength and conditioning program, which uses highly varied, random functional movements performed at a high level of intensity. CrossFit delivers a fitness program, which is broad, general and inclusive. Our specialty is not specializing. The rewards of this program are evidenced in those people participating in combat, survival, sports and all facets of life. This fitness program punishes the specialist!

We are listing several exercises and workouts that we have used with great success. We challenge you to select any random exercises that you can, apply a series of repetitions and rounds to make a fantastic workout. Try to change your workouts often and don't forget to throw in some rest days to recover. The routines that we have placed here are just guidelines. The possibilities are endless depending on what equipment you have available. When possible, try to workout in groups to add a little friendly competition to see who can complete them the fastest or get the most repetitions.

Look at fitness as a sport in itself. Train hard, intense and heavy when possible.

A note of caution as you begin: Start small, some of these routines can cause serious injury or prolonged soreness. Do not try to start a new fitness program such as this right off the bat. Take some time so that your body conditions to the intense stresses placed upon it. The idea is to get fit, not hurt, so start slowly and build your intensity. Last but not least have fun. www.crossfitnc.com

BODY WEIGHT WORKOUTS:

Complete as many rounds as possible in 20 minutes. 5 pull-ups 10 push-ups 20 squats.	Tabata this: Tabata's are 20 sec of work followed by 10 sec of rest. Repeat for 4 minutes. (8 rounds) Your score for each exercise is the least number of reps you completed in 1 round. Finish 1 exercise before moving on. Squats Push-ups Sit ups Pull-ups Burpee's	Complete for best time: Run 400m 50 squats Run 400m 50 push-ups Run 400m 50 pull-ups Run 400m 50 sit ups.	Go through each exercise complete them in order and then move to the next set of repetitions. 21-18-15-9. Complete for time: Dips Squats Push-ups Box Jumps 24" box Pull-ups
Perform 25-20-15-10-5 reps for time: Bag hops Plyometric push-ups Sit-ups	Mark out 4 stations on the ground approx 30' apart to create a suicide course. The repetitions for the exercises are 21 repetitions. Suicide/Burpee Suicide/Squat Suicide/Push-Ups Suicide/ Sit-ups.	An adaptation of CrossFit's famous "Fight Gone Bad". We call this "Fight Gone Military". Count the total number of repetitions you complete of each exercise. Each station is 1 minute. Go for a total score. Push-ups Rope Climbs Squats Burpee Box Jumps	Repeat 3 times Run 800m 5 rope climbs 30 push ups 30 squats.

Box Jump

Chin up

Push up

 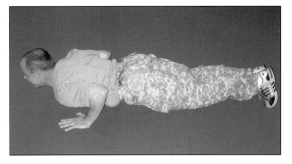

Rope climb leg out　　　　　　**Rope climb leg down**

Versatile

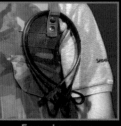

Easy to carry

Fits Channel Pocket

Double Locking

Secures Feet

THE CUFF OF THE FUTURE
SPIDER-Ti ®
HUMAN RESTRAINT SYSTEM
Patented 6,151,761 & 5,651,376
Others Pending

Designed by
Greg Thompson

WWW.SPIDERTI.COM

FEATURES

*Cost effective

*The most versatile restraint on the planet

* Double locking head for extra strength

* Disposable can still be reused

* No Keys, removes quickly with cutters

* 27"Spider-ti is great for securing
legs in a scramble

Chain shackles can
be compromising to
an officer. Spider-Ti
secures legs, limits
legs upward move-
ment, while allowing
prisoner to walk.

Secures hands for transport line,
chain gang or emergency evacuations.
The large loop between wrist allows you to
separate pairs from the group for getting
on and off bus with out having to cut off
the restraints.

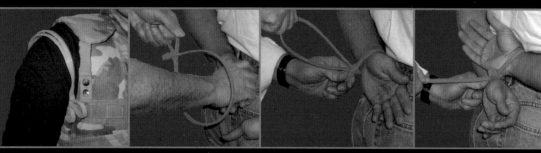

Carry on your shoulder. Slide down your arm onto suspects wrist. Secure both wrists.

DEFENSEBAND™
THE ULTIMATE SELF-DEFENSE WATCH BAND

Designed by
Greg Thompson

Apply standing or on the ground, looks like any normal band, fits any watch. The Heavy-duty Defenseband on your wrist makes it easily accessible. The Defenseband has several ways of applying a vascular restraint as well as securing an arm to prevent an assailant from reaching for other weapons.

Pepper spray, Stun guns, and batons are very common intermediate weapons and self defense devices. They are used because guns and knives are too lethal, may not be legal, may not be accessible in time of need, or may be used against you. For instance if the assailant is on drugs, enraged, or has a resistant body type the intermediate weapons of self defense and other techniques may not be effective.

When applied correctly the DEFENSEBAND will shut off the blood flow temporarily which will make it 100% reliable on anyone at anytime. The DEFENSEBAND on your wrist makes it easily accessible. The DEFENSEBAND has several ways of applying a vascular restraint as well as securing the arm to prevent an assailant from reaching for other weapons.

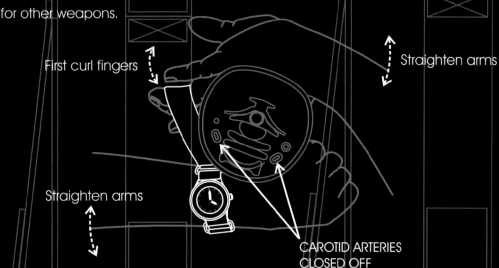

First curl fingers

Straighten arms

Straighten arms

CAROTID ARTERIES
CLOSED OFF

www.defenseband.com

PAT.PENDING

1

2

3

A WATCH BAND THAT WORKS LIKE A SLEEVE CHOKE!

NOTES